The Economy of Medieval Wales, 1067–1536

The Economy of Medieval Wales 1067–1536

MATTHEW FRANK STEVENS

UNIVERSITY OF WALES PRESS
2019

© Matthew Frank Stevens, 2019

All rights reserved. No part of this book may be reproduced in any material form (including photocopying or storing it in any medium by electronic means and whether or not transiently or incidentally to some other use of this publication) without the written permission of the copyright owner except in accordance with the provisions of the Copyright, Designs and Patents Act 1988. Applications for the copyright owner's written permission to reproduce any part of this publication should be addressed to The University of Wales Press, University Registry, King Edward VII Avenue, Cardiff CF10 3NS

www.uwp.co.uk

British Library Cataloguing-in-Publication Data
A catalogue record for this book is available from the British Library.

ISBN: 978-1-78683-484-3
e-ISBN: 978-1-78683-485-0

The right of Matthew Frank Stevens to be identified as author of this work has been asserted by him in accordance with sections 77 and 79 of the Copyright, Designs and Patents Act 1988.

This book is a substantial expansion of a chapter in a forthcoming volume to be published by Brill, *A Companion to Medieval Wales*, ed. Emma Cavell and Kathryn Hurlock (Brill: Leiden and Boston), forthcoming.

Typeset by Chris Bell, cbdesign
Printed by CPI Antony Rowe, Melksham

CONTENTS

Preface vii

Abbreviations ix

Maps xi

Introduction 1

1 Early History, Conquest and Colonisation, 1067–1315 13

2 The Medieval Economy at its Apex, 1282–1348 53

3 Crises and Restructuring, 1315–1536 77

4 Modelling the Economy of Medieval Wales 105

Bibliography 127

Index 143

PREFACE

As an undergraduate student at the University of Wales, Aberystwyth, as it was then known, I had the good fortune to take a final-year course on Welsh society in the later Middle Ages, taught by Dr Llinos Smith, which dealt directly or indirectly with most aspects of the economy of medieval Wales. When appointed lecturer at Swansea University in 2010, I revived Llinos's course, by then having become acquainted with the broader tapestry of pre-modern economic history. This acquaintance had come about through my PhD studies at Aberystwyth with Professor Phillipp Schofield, and my postdoctoral research at Oxford University, funded by the Economic History Society, and at the Centre for Metropolitan History, Institute of Historical Research, University of London. Setting about to teach the history of Wales for the first time, I was struck by the general absence of substantive dscussion of Wales within the well-developed historiography of the economy of medieval Britain and Europe. This is not due to a lack of suitable primary source material for study, but, one suspects, due to the view that medieval Wales, with its unfamiliar native social institutions and political fragmentation, is a sort of *terra incognita* when viewed from beyond

Offa's Dyke. However, a great deal of research regarding the economy of medieval Wales, often scattered and overlooked, has been conducted over the past century and more. This book seeks to draw that research together into a sensible narrative, relating it to English and Eopean historiography and making it accessible to students and historians alike.

Pulling this material together, and offering an accessible analysis of it, has been a most challenging task, and the reader must judge for him- or herself the degree of my success. While any failures of the text presented here are the author's alone, several people are owed particular thanks for their advice and assistance in preparing it. Foremost is Professor Stephen Rigby of Manchester University, whose advice to drastically revise the structure of the original draft, and comments on various subsequent drafts, greatly improved the final product. I must also thank Professor David Stephenson, for his comments, and Dr Emma Cavell, who inspired this monograph by prompting me to write a short chapter-length survey of the medieval economy of Wales that grew into the present book. Thanks are due to my other colleagues at Swansea University, not least Professor Martin Johns and Dr John Law and, keeping with custom, my undergraduate students of the course 'Welsh Society in the Later Middle Ages'. Support for the completion of this project was provided by Swansea University, in the form of sabbatical leave, the British Academy (grant no.SG171150, 'Jim Crow in Medieval Wales: a comparative approach to the long history of legal discrimination and segregation') and the National Science Centre, Poland (Narodowe Centrum Nauki: project no. UMO-2016/22/M/HS3/00157, 'Social and political order of the communal towns in the European peripheries from the 12th to the 16th c.', principal investigator, Professor Roman Czaja, Uniwersytet Mikołaja Kopernika, Toruń). Thanks are also due to my parents and Patricia Henninger, who have kindly supported my studies.

For Monika

ABBREVIATIONS

AgeCon.	R. R. Davies, *The Age of Conquest: Wales, 1067–1415* (Oxford, 1995)
AgHist.	*The Agrarian History of England and Wales*, 8 vols (Cambridge, 1939–81)
BBCS	*Bulletin of the Board of Celtic Studies*
Boroughs	R. A. Griffiths (ed.), *Boroughs of Medieval Wales* (Cardiff, 1978)
DHST	*Denbighshire Historical Society Transactions*
EcHR	*The Economic History Review*
GlamCH	T. B. Pugh (ed.), *Glamorgan County History, vol. III: The Middle Ages* (Cardiff, 1971)
GwentCH	R. A. Griffiths, T. Hopkins and R. Howell (eds), *The Gwent County History, vol. II: The Age of the Marcher Lords, c.1070–1536* (Cardiff, 2008)
LordSoc.	R. R. Davies, *Lordship and Society in the March of Wales, 1282–1400* (Oxford, 1978)
NLWJ	*National Library of Wales Journal*
P&P	*Past and Present*

SouthWales	W. Rees, *South Wales and the March, 1284–1415: A Social and Agrarian Study* (Oxford, 1924)
Statutes	I. Bowen (ed.), *The Statutes of Wales* (London, 1908)
Towns	I. Soulsby, *The Towns of Medieval Wales: A Study of their History, Archaeology and Early Topography* (Chichester, 1983)
TransAng.	*Transactions of the Anglesey Antiquarian Society and Field Club*
TransCymm.	*Transactions of the Honourable Society of Cymmrodorion*
TransRoyal	*Transactions of the Royal Historical Society*
UrbanCult.	H. Fulton (ed.), *Urban Culture in Medieval Wales* (Cardiff, 2012)
WelshSoc.	T. Jones Pierce, *Medieval Welsh Society: Selected Essays*, ed. J. B. Smith (Cardiff, 1972)
WHR	*Welsh History Review*

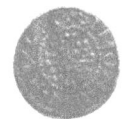

MAPS[1]

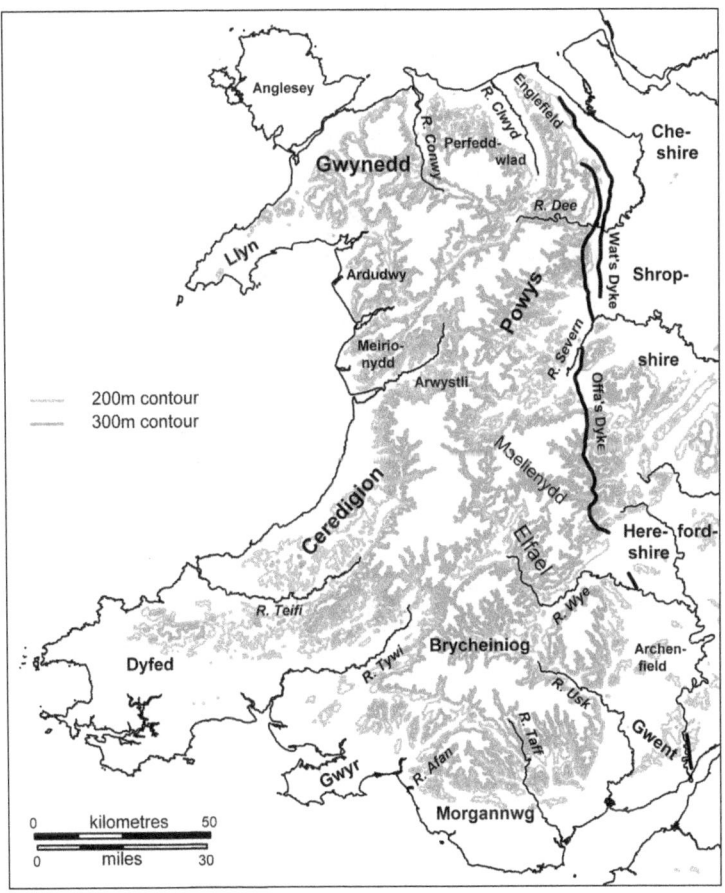

Map 1. *Wales and its borders in the eleventh century.*

---

[1]Maps 1 and 2 are reproduced from M. Lieberman, *The March of Wales, 1067–1300* (Cardiff, 2008), pp. 129–30; Every effort has been made to secure permission to reprint them here.

Map 2. The Principality and March of Wales in the fourteenth century.

Maps xiii

Map 3. The towns of fourteenth-century Wales.

INTRODUCTION

THERE IS NO general survey of the economy of medieval Wales. As a result, there is no equivalent to Jim Bolton's masterful and often strongly data-driven *The Medieval English Economy, 1150–1500* (1980), nor to Edward Miller and John Hatcher's two volumes on the English economy from 1086 to 1348, *Medieval England: Rural Society and Economic Change* (1978) and *Medieval England: Towns, Commerce and Crafts* (1995).[1] Some books, such as Michael Postan's classic *The Medieval Economy and Society: An Economic History of Britain in the Middle Ages* (*c*.400–1500; first published 1972), do feature 'Britain' in their title. Yet Postan's study is typical in that the terms 'Wales' and 'Welsh' garner just seven indexed entries from among 281 pages of text, five of which are passing references to Wales as a liminal place bounding the area under discussion.[2] Among surveys by prominent economic historians writing about late medieval 'Britain' in recent decades, only Richard Britnell's *Britain and Ireland, 1050–1530* stands out as making a concerted and somewhat effective effort to incorporate Welsh data. Christopher Dyer's *Making a Living in the Middle Ages: The people of Britain, 850–1520* discusses some Welsh evidence, but delivers an overall narrative based on England.³ Most recently, *British Economic Growth, 1270–1870* by Stephen Broadberry, Bruce Campbell and others, excludes medieval Wales and Scotland for reasons that are not made clear, and unabashedly considers only England for the period before 1700, turning to Britain as a whole for the eighteenth and nineteenth centuries.⁴

The inevitable problem with such works, for the historian of Wales, Ireland or Scotland, is that they focus, of necessity, on the historical framework that is best applicable to the two-thirds of the perhaps nine million people of medieval Britain (including Ireland $c.$1300, when population was at its peak) who lived in England.⁵ The net result is a narrative that looks at Wales, Ireland and Scotland (and, indeed even upland England) from the outside, and tends to compress, by identifying similarities between these areas, their stories into a secondary thread woven into the main lowland-England narrative. For example, Britnell's excellent study of over 500 pages cites Welsh evidence in about 100 instances, weaving Wales into its narrative of Britain and Ireland's economic and demographic growth from 1050 to 1314, and their economic restructuring and demographic decline and stagnation in the fourteenth and fifteenth centuries. However, the Welsh material is typically cited as supporting evidence to extend broader narratives into Wales, thereby tying the experience of Wales to that of the other largely upland, pastoral zones of Scotland, Ireland and north-west England.⁶ Rarely is sufficient detail given which would allow a substantive discussion of Welsh development in its own right.⁷ Often this is understandable given that Wales accounted for perhaps only 3–4 per cent of Britain's population, $c.$1300, no more than 300,000 at most.⁸ But it can also be highly misleading since, as we shall see below, the nature, chronology and causes of economic change could often differ between Wales and other parts of the British Isles (see Chapter 4, 'Modelling the Economy of Medieval Wales').

Wales is a small nation and few historians have served its medieval history. Fewer still have served its economic history, especially regarding the period following the so-called 'final conquest' of 1282. Only Antony Carr's brief thematic chapter in Stephen Rigby's *A Companion* to Britain in the Later Middle Ages *offers a general survey of the economy of later medieval Wales for the modern student.[9] In this, Carr adopts uncritically the approach of post-World War II scholars that economic change in Wales was demographically driven, reinforced by more recent historiographical trends towards environmental determinism (see below, and Chapter 4).[10] He writes, 'The primary cause of economic change in Wales was the rise in population, the result of a period of favourable climate between about 1050 and 1300. The statistical basis for estimates of population range from the extremely tenuous to the non-existent.'[11] Subsequent developments, from the mid-fourteenth century, are then attributed to population decline.[12] That is to say, Carr takes a specific approach, heavily dependent on the key variable of population, which he does not scrutinise. Overall, what research there has been on the economy of medieval Wales has been both thematically discontinuous and geographically and chronologically uneven in coverage.

The first pioneers of the economic history of Wales, around the turn of the nineteenth and twentieth centuries, were interested in commerce, and the political institutions and social structures that gave way to its growth and elaboration. While Sir John Edward Lloyd (1861–1947) is often cited as the 'father' of academic Welsh history, both medieval and national, on account of his landmark two-volume *A History of Wales* published in 1911, his contemporary Edward Lewis (1880–1942) ought rightly to be considered the 'father' of the economic history of Wales.[13] Lewis's extended 1903 essay on 'The Development of Industry and Commerce in Wales During the Middle Ages', and his 1912 monograph, *The Medieval Boroughs of Snowdonia*, remain fundamental to modern scholarship.[14] Unlike Lloyd, who studied at Oxford, Lewis was a product of the recently formed London School of Economics (LSE), where he drafted his work on *The Medieval Boroughs* in candidature for his doctorate before departing for the University of Wales, Aberystwyth in 1910.[15] Two years later, when Lewis's book was published, LSE admitted William Rees (1887–1978), who in 1924 produced the first detailed monograph on the medieval Welsh rural economy: *South Wales and the March, 1284–1415*.[16] Rees, influenced by the new holistic approach of the French *Annales* school, also produced a four-sheet map of 'South Wales and the March in the fourteenth century', garnering international praise.[17] Lewis and Rees, who were associated with Lloyd by way of the History and Law Committee of the University of Wales's Board of Celtic Studies, examined the commercialisation of Wales in the wake of the English conquest, working from the records created by 'Norman' and 'English' administrators.[18] Historians tend to speak of 'Norman' conquest and leadership in the eleventh and early twelfth centuries, and 'English' conquest and leadership from the later twelfth century, especially after English King John's loss of Normandy in 1204. The distinction is vague, based on fluid notions of identity among what would remain a French-speaking elite into the fourteenth century.

By contrast, the economic history of Wales in the period before conquest only blossomed after World War II. In the late nineteenth century, Fredrick Seebohm (1833–1912), in *The Tribal System in Wales*, had used post-conquest records to attempt to derive the nature and structures of native Welsh society, but his problematic assumptions about the primitive nature of native society had served only to close the subject (see below) until it was re-examined by Thomas Jones Pierce (1905–64). Jones Pierce's brilliant but densely written studies of native systems of taxation, administration and law were, like Rees's work, influenced by aspects of the *Annales* school's concern for landscapes and mentalities, but they appeared across scattered publications and were only brought together after his death, in the 1972 volume *Medieval Welsh Society*.[19] Jones Pierce's last work was published in *The Agrarian History of England and Wales*, volume one (1972; part one).[20] In the same volume (part two) there appeared an extended essay by his student, historical geographer Glanville Jones (1923–96), who advanced, for Wales, the *Annales*-style investigation of interaction between geography and society.[21] Jones's work, especially on medieval Anglesey, established the pattern of medieval Welsh settlement expansion, affirmed the presence and importance of unfree tenants under native lordship, and corrected many of Seebohm's mischaracterisations of the Welsh.[22]

The Agrarian History of England and Wales, especially volumes one (part two), two and three, published between 1972 and 1991, includes the most comprehensive collection of essays on the economic history of medieval Wales yet published.²³ It also bridges the gap between the *Annales*-orientated writings of those such as Rees, Jones Pierce and Jones, and a new wave of post-1945 research focusing on population, resources, farming techniques, peasant housing and economic change associated, for medieval English history, with the work of Michael Postan and his followers.²⁴ The first three volumes of *The Agrarian History* contain 309 pages on these topics by Jones Pierce, Ian Jack, Huw Owen and Lawrence Butler.²⁵ Huw Owen's chapters on land occupation, farming and the tenantry of Wales after 1348, in volume three of *The Agrarian History*, are of particular importance, as the later-fourteenth and fifteenth centuries especially have been neglected by historians.²⁶

The 1970s to 1990s also saw considerable work, published in article and chapter form, on post-conquest seigniorial incomes and administration by Sir Rees Davies, Llinos Smith and others.²⁷ Urbanisation in Wales re-emerged as a topic of interest in the late 1970s, with Ralph Griffiths's edited volume *Boroughs of Wales* and Ian Soulsby's foundational gazetteer of *The Towns of Medieval Wales*, which examined the origins and functions of towns, issues developed more recently in my monograph on Ruthin (Denbighshire) and Helen Fulton's edited volume assessing the nature of *Urban Culture in Medieval Wales*.²⁸ Most recently, trade networks between Wales and England, a topic largely neglected since Lewis's time, have begun to receive new attention, prompted in part by the discovery of a well-preserved section of fifteenth-century ship's hull in Newport (Gwent).²⁹

This brief survey of the historiography of the economy of medieval Wales shows that historians have addressed a wide range of topics and produced a number of important studies. Nevertheless work in this field remains patchy, particularly in comparison with the rich literature on medieval England. Thus, whereas the English content of *The Agrarian History* volumes comprises as series of informative surveys that draw on thousands of pages of previously published research, the Welsh chapters constitute unique cornerstones of knowledge in their own right. Many key topics of medieval Welsh social and economic history are still only represented by a single work. For instance, the only attempt to reconstruct the pre-conquest organisation of the kingdom of Deheubarth remains the body of Jones Pierce's work in *Medieval Welsh Society*.[30] The only serious attempt to calculate medieval population in Wales is Keith Williams-Jones's introduction to *The Merioneth Lay Subsidy Roll*.[31] The only in-depth study of the economy of a medieval Welsh town is my monograph on Ruthin[32] Perhaps even more surprisingly, the only general study of the impact of the Black Death in Wales remains William Rees's twenty-page article in the 1920 *Transitions of the Royal Historical Society*. As illustrated by the above, the general topics investigated and approaches employed by historians of Wales have often mirrored international historiographical trends. Yet the continued lack of a critical mass of work in most areas of the economic history of Wales inhibits the scope for comparison and debate regarding Welsh evidence in its own right, without the need to co-opt non-Welsh – usually English – evidence and historiography. This has the potential to produce misleading results. At the same time, historians of pre-modern England and 'Britain', as discussed above, tend to eschew Welsh evidence as arising from an academic *terra incognita*, or to extend Anglocentric narratives to Wales uncritically.

Given the lack of general surveys of medieval Welsh economic history, it is tempting for scholars to make sense of the broad arc of Welsh economic history by adopting the narratives of development that have been established for medieval England and are summarised in John Hatcher and Mark Bailey's excellent *Modelling the Middle Ages*.[33] Certainly, many of the trends that they identify for England, such as the economic expansion of the period from 1066 to 1348, driven by population growth, commercialisation and the decanting of landless peasants into growing urban communities, and the subsequent depopulation, Anglo-French war and urban decline in the later fourteenth and fifteenth centuries, hold true for Wales. Yet such similarities are often deceptive and the details sometimes radically different. For instance, as we shall see below, population growth was augmented by English invasion and immigration, urban expansion was a direct result of Norman and English town plantation, and the war that tipped the Welsh economy into precipitous decline was the destructive revolt of Owain

Glyndŵr, rather than the Hundred Years' War. Moreover, a distinctive theme of Welsh medieval history is the decline and disappearance of native social and economic structures under the impact of English settlement and conquest. It is with these divergences in mind, as much as the similarities to English developments, that this book seeks to outline the economic history and historiography of Wales across the entire high and late medieval period, from 1067 to 1536, and to consider the extent to which models of medieval international and English developments can usefully be applied to medieval Wales.

Chapters one to three of the book offer a largely narrative history of the economy of Wales, from the Anglo-Norman invasion (1067) and creation of a marcher economy, to the union of England and Wales in 1536. Economies, and the societies that they reflect, constantly evolve, and trends in agriculture, lordship, trade or any other aspect of an economy almost invariably lack clear-cut beginnings and ends. This means that the date ranges employed in labelling the chapters that follow are only indicative, and it is often necessary to stray across the arbitrary chronological boundaries chosen as much for their convenience as their economic significance.

Chapter one sets out the nature of Welsh economic and social systems at the time of the Anglo-Norman invasion of south-east Wales in 1067, identifying the earlier origins of demographic and economic trends when necessary and assessing the impacts of invasion and colonisation through the completion of the conquest of Wales in 1282 to the onset of the Great Famine of 1315–22. Chapter two offers a snapshot of the medieval economy at its apex, between the conquest of 1282 and the Great Famine, indicating the patterns of industry and commerce, urbanisation and economic lordship that had by then emerged and that would be carried forward into the later-fourteenth and fifteenth centuries. Chapter three surveys the decline and restructuring of the economy between 1315–22 and the Acts of Union of England and Wales of 1536, including the calamitous Black Death from 1348–9 and revolt of Owain Glyndŵr from 1400. Chapter four, in lieu of a traditional conclusion summarising the empirical history presented here, offers a more theoretical approach to the subject of medieval economic and social change in Wales. It asks to what extent the major theories (the neo-Malthusian, neo-Marxist and commercialisation models) that historians have used to make sense of medieval economic change can be used to make sense of developments in Wales. The volume thus seeks to provide a critical synthesis of existing work on the economy of medieval Wales, from the early twentieth century to present, and to advance beyond it. But, above all, its goals are to promote discussion and to stimulate further research, and to show that the economy of Wales is a worthy and invigorating area of study in its own right.

Notes

1. J. Bolton, *The Medieval English Economy, 1150–1500* (London, 1980); E. Miller and J. Hatcher, *Medieval England: Rural Society and Economic Change, 1086–1348* (London, 1978); E. Miller and J. Hatcher, *Medieval England: Towns, Commerce, and Crafts, 1086–1348* (London, 1995).
2. M. M. Postan, *The Medieval Economy and Society: An Economic History of Britain in the Middle Ages* (London, 1972; Harmondsworth, 1975), pp. 3, 6, 12, 13, 97, 102, 127.
3. R. Britnell, *Britain and Ireland, 1050–1530* (Oxford, 2004); C. Dyer, *Making a Living in the Middle Ages: The People of Britain, 850–1520* (London, 2002); S. H. Rigby, '[Book review] Christopher Dyer, *Making a Living in the Middle Ages: The People of Britain, 850–1520*', *Social History*, 15 (1990), 111–14.
4. S. Broadberry, B. M. S. Campbell, A. Klein, M. Overton and B. van Leeuwen, *British Economic Growth, 1270–1870* (Cambridge, 2015).
5. Broadberry et al., *British Economic Growth*, p. 81.
6. Examples are legion. For instance, Britnell, *Britain and Ireland*, pp. 27 (lordship in Wales and Ireland), 58 (Welsh and northern English judicial independence), 214, 216 (sheep farming in Wales, Scotland and the north of England); 329 (Irish and Welsh benefit from high English tariffs).

7   Britnell, *Britain and Ireland*, pp. 8–10, 38–9, 58, 61, 104–5, 129–32; 164–5, 174, 198, 209–13, 230–1, 234–8, 272–4, 368–9, 376–9, 434, 441–2, 444–5, 482–5, 495–6.
8   Britnell, *Britain and Ireland*, p. 81.
9   A. D. Carr, 'Wales: economy and society', in S. H. Rigby (ed.), *A Companion to Britain in the Later Middle Ages* (Oxford, 2003), pp. 125–41.
10 On the role of environment see, B. Campbell, *The Great Transition: Climate, Disease and Society in the Late-Medieval World* (Cambridge, 2016), esp. pp. 1–24.
11 Carr, 'Wales: economy and society', p. 126.
12 Carr, 'Wales: economy and society', pp. 133–7.
13 J. E. Lloyd, *A History of Wales from the Earliest Times to the Edwardian Conquest*, 2 vols (London, 1911); H. Pryce, *J. E. Lloyd and the Creation of Welsh History: Renewing a Nation's Past* (Cardiff, 2011).
14 E. A. Lewis, 'The development of industry and commerce in Wales during the Middle Ages', *TransRoyal*, new series, 17 (1903), 121–73; E. A. Lewis, *The Medieval Boroughs of Snowdonia* (London, 1912).
15 Lewis, *The Medieval Boroughs of Snowdonia*, p. v.
16 R. A. Griffiths, 'William Rees and the modern study of medieval Wales', in R. A. Griffiths and P. R. Schofield (eds), *Wales and the Welsh in the Middle Ages: Essays Presented to J. Beverly Smith* (Cardiff, 2011), pp. 206–7; W. Rees, *South Wales and the March, 1284–1415: A Social and Agrarian Study* (Oxford, 1924).
17 Griffiths, 'William Rees', p. 213; W. Rees, 'South Wales and the March in the fourteenth century', map, four sheets (Ordinance Survey, 1933).
18 Griffiths, 'William Rees', p. 215.
19 T. Jones Pierce, *Medieval Welsh Society: Selected Essays*, ed. J. B. Smith (Cardiff, 1972), 'Introduction', pp. 11–17.
20 T. Jones Pierce, 'Landlords in Wales, nobility and gentry', in H. P. R. Finberg (ed.), *AgHist.*, vol. IV: *1500–1640* (Cambridge, 1967), pp. 357–81.
21 G. R. J. Jones, 'Post-Roman Wales', in H. P. R. Finberg (ed.), *AgHist.*, vol. I, part II: *A.D. 43–1042* (Cambridge, 1972), pp. 283–382.
22 G. R. J. Jones, 'The Distribution of Medieval Settlement in Anglesey', *TransAng.* (1955), 27–96.; G. R. J. Jones, 'The Tribal System in Wales: A Re-assessment in the Light of Settlement Studies', *WHR*, 1 (1960–3), 111–32.

23 Finberg (ed.), *AgHist.*, vol. I, part II: *A.D. 43–1042*; H. E. Hallam (ed.), *AgHist.*, vol. II: *1042–1350* (Cambridge, 1988); E. Miller (ed.) *AgHist.*, vol. III: *1348–1500* (Cambridge, 1991).

24 For an international context and more generally, see M. M. Postan (ed.), *The Cambridge Economic History of Europe, vol. I: The Agrarian Life of the Middle Ages*, 2nd edn (Cambridge, 1972).

25 Jones, 'Post-Roman Wales', in Finberg (ed.), *AgHist.*, vol. I, part II, pp. 283–382; R. I. Jack, 'New settlement: H Wales and the Marches', in Hallam (ed.), *AgHist.*, vol. II, pp. 260–71; R. I. Jack, 'I. Farming techniques: H Wales and the Marches', in Hallam (ed.), *AgHist.*, vol. II, pp. 412–96; R. I. Jack, 'Social structure: H Wales and the Marches', in Hallam (ed.), *AgHist.*, vol. II, pp. 699–714; Butler, 'Wales', in Hallam (ed.), *AgHist.*, vol. II, pp. 933–65; D. H. Owen, 'The occupation of the land: F Wales and the Marches', in Miller (ed.), *AgHist.*, vol. III, pp. 92–106; D. H. Owen, 'Farming practice and techniques: F Wales and the Marches', in Miller (ed.), *AgHist.*, vol. III, pp. 238–54; D. H. Owen, 'Tenant farming and tenant farmers: F Wales and the Marches', in Miller (ed.), *AgHist.*, vol. III, pp. 648–61; Butler, 'Rural building in England and Wales: Wales', in Miller (ed.), *AgHist.*, vol. III, pp. 894–919 ; See, for comparison, M. M. Postan, 'England', in Postan (ed.), *The Cambridge Economic History*, vol. I, pp., 549–632.

26 Owen, 'The occupation of the land', pp. 92–106; Owen, 'Farming practice and techniques', pp. 238–54; Owen, 'Tenant farming and tenant farmers', pp. 648–61.

27 For example, *LordSoc.*, chapter 8, 'The profits of lordship', pp. 176–98; Ll. B. Smith, 'Seignorial Income in the Fourteenth Century: The Arundels in Chirk', *BBCS*, 28 (1979), 443–57; J. Given, 'The Economic Consequences of the English Conquest of Gwynedd', *Speculum*, 74 (1989), 11–45.

28 R.A.Griffiths (ed.), *Boroughs of Medieval Wales* (Cardiff, 1978); I. Soulsby, *The Towns of Medieval Wales: A Study of their History, Archaeology and Early Topography* (Chichester, 1983); M. F. Stevens, *Urban Assimilation in Post-Conquest Wales: Ethnicity, Gender and Economy in Ruthin, 1282–1348* (Cardiff, 2010); H. Fulton (ed.), *Urban Culture in Medieval Wales* (Cardiff, 2012).

29 E. T. Jones and R. Stone (eds), *The World of the Newport Medieval Ship: Trade, Politics and Shipping in the Mid-fifteenth Century* (Cardiff, 2018).
30 *WelshSoc*
31 K. Williams-Jones, *The Merioneth Lay Subsidy Roll, 1292–3* (Cardiff, 1976).
32 Stevens, *Urban Assimilation*.
33 J. Hatcher and M. Bailey, *Modelling the Middle Ages: The History and Theory of England's Economic Development* (Oxford, 2001).

Chapter one
EARLY HISTORY, CONQUEST AND COLONISATION, 1067–1315

The organisation of native society to *c*.1100

WALES WAS, by the eleventh century, divided into a number of competing kingdoms. The most notable of these were Gwynedd in the north-west, Powys in east central Wales, Morgannwg (also called Glywysing) in the south-east and Deheubarth (that is, the kingdom of Dyfed plus other realms of the royal house of Dinefwr) in south-west Wales.[1] The rulers of these kingdoms, typically styled 'princes' in recognition of the modest extent of their realms, competed for control over a hierarchy of administrative-territorial units: the cantref, the commote and the *maenor* (plural *maenorau*).[2] These units existed from at least the conception of the body of Welsh law attributed to the mid-tenth-century prince of Deheubarth, Hywel Dda ap Cadell (d. 949/950), which, through the work of many hands, would evolve over many generations to become the regionally varied but universally recognised law of native Wales. The concept of lordship in native society primarily reflected a concern for the establishment and maintenance of hierarchies of dependence between and within descent groups of related free men who controlled the territorial units they occupied, and between those groups and the prince.[3] Lordship as a mechanism for the direct control of land and collection renders and services, with the prince as the greatest lord, was developing from the twelfth century with the introduction of concepts of feudalism.[4] By the thirteenth century close colleagues and social peers of the Welsh rulers were interjecting themselves, as lords with local territorial control, between their dependants and the princes.[5]

The geographical size of medieval territorial units and the number of their constituent subdivisions was highly variable. Typically, the more productive and more densely populated the unit was, the smaller was its geographical extent. For example, Anglesey, which was highly productive and densely populated by Welsh standards, was divided into three cantrefs, each comprising two commotes.[6] By comparison, cantrefs spanning mountainous areas, such as Cantref Mawr (literally 'the big cantref') containing seven commotes and situated between the Black Mountains and historic Cardiganshire, were twice as large as those on Anglesey.[7]

Until about the year 1100, taxation was based on the *maenor*. A *maenor* was a flexible territorial unit comprising about a third or a quarter of a commote, and supplied either labour and food renders or a *gwestfa* tribute to the Welsh prince or lord.[8] Local records of the administrative workings of commotes and *maenorau* do not exist, but *maenorau* are described in an idealised form in Welsh law books. These suggest that there were mainly arable *maenorau* of unfree peasants, notionally containing seven *trefi*, and mainly pastoral *maenorau* of free persons, notionally containing thirteen *trefi*; a *tref* equated loosely to an English vill or township, and could refer elastically to a nucleated village of clustered houses or an area of dispersed farmsteads.[9] An unfree *maenor* was typically populated by persons living in houses clustered around arable fields of *tir cyfrif*, or 'shareland', distributed among and cultivated by unfree peasants who rendered to the prince or lord various labour services, such as carriage of goods and harvest work, and agricultural produce. A free *maenor* typically comprised dispersed settlements and, while not without arable lands, contained a greater focus on animal husbandry. A free *maenor* notionally provided a *gwestfa*, or tribute, from the resident free extended-family grouping(s) to the prince or lord, taking various forms. The *gwestfa* was recorded in thirteenth-century Cardiganshire, for example, as entertainment for the lord and his entourage – primarily food – four times annually.¹⁰ The *gwestfa* would have been subdivided among liable *trefi* of free families and was in later centuries commuted (see below) to a notional cash sum called the *twnc* pound.¹¹

A tripartite administrative apparatus tended to exist in each commote, consisting of a local *llys*, or hall, *tir bwrdd*, or a demesne farm belonging to the prince or lord, and a *maerdref*, or village occupied by unfree peasants charged with carrying out menial maintenance tasks in and about the court.¹² The *llys* was the meeting place of the court, in both the social and judicial sense of the term, a collection point of unfree renders and prooobably of payments associated with the *gwestfa* and *twnc* tribute. This apparatus was notionally overseen, according to some law books, by a centrally appointed local official called a *maer*, or land *maer biswail* (literally dung-*maer*).¹³

In the century and a half after 1100 a number of other officers and their economic functions would be associated with the *llys-maerdref* complex. Of ancient origin and continued significance beyond English conquest (see below), are the *rhaglaw*, or 'bailiff', and *rhinghel*, or 'beadle'. The *rhaglaw* was the chief official of the territorial ruler, later records suggesting he collected rents, issued summonses, arrested suspected felons and oversaw purveyance, the compulsory purchase of supplies.¹⁴ The *rhingyll* was, at least initially, an inferior officer to the *rhaglaw* who dealt with the unfree concerning various dues and renders, but who in later centuries became the more responsible official and chief arm of royal government.¹⁵ A number of other officials, with less overtly economic roles, can also be found in the Welsh law books.

Three key points are to be taken away from this outline of the administrative and social institutions that framed the Welsh agrarian economy before 1100. First, Wales was governed through structures that were scaled to their economic output, as shown by the varying size of commotes in relation to their fertility and population. Second, social structures were designed to maximise economic output, with denser unfree communities tied to the best lowland arable, and more dispersed free communities extending into upland areas that they exploited through pastoral animal husbandry. Third, the presence of officials provided by the prince or lord to oversee these social structures, enforcing the labour services of the unfree *maenorau* and collecting the *gwestfa* tribute of the free *maenorau*, indicates an effort to maintain and promote the agrarian system. Native Wales had a carefully managed, if not necessarily centrally planned, agrarian economy.

Urban life, in contrast, was not developed by native rulers until long after 1100. In Roman times, the native inhabitants of Wales could not but have been aware of commerce and towns. Roman forts across Wales, in particular at Caernarfon, Cardiff and, most importantly, Caerleon, were supported by trading settlements and remained or were renewed as foci of political control in the early Middle Ages. At Caerleon, a Roman garrison of 6,000 soldiers was supported by an extensive civilian community, and early Welsh rulers subsequently occupied and fortified the site until its eventual Norman takeover and commercial revival in the twelfth century.[16] But unlike in England and northern Europe, where a degree of urban or proto-urban life survived the end of Roman rule, the fifth-century withdrawal of Roman troops from Wales heralded the all but total collapse of any clearly 'urban' commerce.[17] The use of coinage as a means of exchange declined sharply, and ceased in most areas.[18] At the turn of the eleventh century Welsh society was under the sway of a competitive ruling class of warrior freemen who governed their small kingdoms through the ideological prism of 'heroic values and aggressive militarism'.[19] Pillage, plunder and tribute taking were the norm, making permanent or large-scale trading settlements unsustainable targets. The agricultural surpluses of peasant production that, in England, might have gone to market, were largely collected and consumed or redistributed by Welsh rulers on progress throughout their dominions. Wendy Davies has argued that commercial exchange in Wales before 1070 was unusually small by European standards, focused on the import of small quantities of luxury goods such as silks or wine, and orientated towards the sea trade that circulated between Bristol, Ireland and Chester.[20] Some long-distance overland trade to England may well have existed but was 'probably not great' and focused on 'necessities', such as foodstuffs.²¹ From the eleventh century, native rulers moved slowly in the direction of the more systematic exploitation of their economic resources in response to, or in 'dialogue' with, their new Anglo-Norman neighbours.²² Most importantly, economic development in Wales was frequently prompted by violent interaction with Anglo-Norman leaders, until by the later thirteenth century the pace and extent of change was such that even native rulers were carried along.

In a sequence of events indicative of the long-term pattern of conflict and development to follow, in 1063, Harold Godwinson, Earl of Wessex and future king of England, defeated Gruffydd ap Llywelyn, ruler of much of Wales, and in the summer of 1065 built a fortified burh at Portskewett, in Gwent.²³ This was probably intended as a protected commercial centre for English merchants on the western shore of the *Môr Hafren*, or 'Severn Sea', known in English since the sixteenth century as the Bristol Channel. Within weeks, the fledgling initiative was sacked by the new king of Gwent, Caradog ap Gruffudd. But Caradog's counteroffensive would only inspire a stronger invasion. Harold's claims in Gwent were renewed by the new Norman Earl of Wessex, William fitz Osbern, when in 1067 he campaigned in Gwent and founded fortified settlements at Monmouth and Chepstow (then called 'Striguil').²⁴ In this way, the characteristic pattern of military-commercial engagement emerged: Anglo-Norman thrust and outpost foundation, Welsh riposte, and, finally, sustained Anglo-Norman counter-attack and occupation with associated settlement. However, towns, markets and coin-hungry local officials – the principal economic elements of this transformation – would have to be protected behind high walls for centuries.

This pattern of interaction between natives and incomers had a profound and transformative effect on Welsh society and the economy in rural Wales well beyond the areas that were coming under direct and durable Anglo-Norman control. Thomas Jones Pierce suggested that Norman power, even in places unadulterated by invasion, 'appears to have exerted indirect pressures which brought about a veritable agrarian revolution in the years between 1100 and 1300'.²⁵ This took place in two phases. The first was a form of internal colonisation, from about

1100, in which free family groupings grew in size and complexity to occupy more fully upland *trefi* and *maenorau*. The second was a form of administrative streamlining, largely eliminating distinctions between unfree and free Welsh, that native rulers undertook upon recovering territories formerly subject to Anglo-Norman control.

The first phase of this 'revolution' involved enhancing the role of the extended family in exploiting only marginally croppable and upland territories. The *gwely* (plural, *gwelyau*), or four-generational agnatic kin group – that is, all men sharing the same great-grandfather – had been the unit of production from time immemorial when Norman lords first reached the Welsh borders. From Roman times, these *gwelyau* units occupied the best-drained soils on the Welsh coastal plains and valley floors, most often as unfree *tir cyfrif* tenants of correspondingly unfree *trefi* and *maenorau*. As the population grew in the absence of additional, fertile arable lands (see below), and as Welsh rulers sought to exploit their estates more fully, *gwelyau* expanded inland and family units adopted a system of transhumance in which time was divided between lowland arable and upland pastoral agriculture. These new secondary settlements tended to be of a free character, although they were sometimes created by the deliberate reorganisation of very small settlements of bondmen on marginal lands who formed semi-free *gwelyau*.[26] The new settlements gave rise to new, mostly free, *trefi* and *maenorau*. The areas occupied by these new extended-family units themselves came to be called *gwelyau*, giving the term both social and territorial meanings. The growth of free *gwelyau* social-territorial units in number and importance started along the north-eastern borderlands early in the twelfth century, gradually spreading west and south until they affected the whole of native Wales.[27] We know little of the exact drivers of this development, and any attempt to articulate this shift artificially imposes a degree of order on a confusedly devolved process. But the new semi-free and free *gwelyau*, as social-territorial units, have been viewed as both 'the core of a more stable agrarian structure' and a mechanism for the better exploitation of resources in response to the rising Anglo-Norman threat.[28]

The second phase of this 'revolution' hinged on the de facto liberation of unfree tenants following intervals of Anglo-Norman control.

Best explored is historic Cardiganshire, roughly corresponding to the Welsh kingdom of Deheubarth, most of which was subject to Anglo-Norman overlordship during the first half of the twelfth century.[29] In Cardiganshire, twelfth-century political disturbances resulted in the extinction or flight of much of the ancient bond population. After Welsh native control was re-established in the later twelfth century, the *gwely*, in its sense as a combined social and territorial unit, grew to underpin the economic organisation of the revived kingdom of Deheubarth. A more or less uniform and streamlined taxation of the land by a reimagined free *gwestfa* tribute, collected in services and goods against relatively regular territorial '*gwestfa*' units, was introduced.[30] The obliteration of unfree communities rendering servile dues and services in favour of tax-paying free *gwelyau* was not entirely complete, with some 'free' *gwelyau* continuing to provide very light services to the prince or lord, such as limited harrowing, reaping and carriage of goods.[31] But the effect, mirrored to a lesser extent throughout other parts of Wales – least strongly in the native stronghold of Gwynedd, where substantial unfree communities remained – was near enough complete to sow confusion regarding the antiquity and extent of unfree communities in the minds of a generation of modern historians of Wales.

During the first half of the twentieth century our understanding of this sequence of events was obscured by the problematic work of Fredrick Arthur Seebohm (d. 1912), published as *The Tribal System in Wales*.[32] Seebohm, working backwards from post-conquest English records of subjugated upland Welsh *gwelyau*, wrongly characterised the Welsh as embodying a timeless society of highly mobile 'tribal' cattle herders, unversed in lowland agriculture. This view was much criticised by Jones Pierce in a series of articles from the 1950s but only conclusively overturned by Glanville Jones in an article published in the 1963 maiden volume of *The Welsh History Review*, demonstrating that Welsh unfree communities were of ancient origin and preceded the growth of free *gwelyau* in the manner set out above. Nevertheless, the classification/characterisation of medieval Wales as 'tribal' has continued, sometimes as a term of convenience and sometimes as a result of Seebohm's lingering influence.[33]

The administrative changes wrought by Anglo-Norman invaders in areas under their direct control were equally revolutionary. These extended well beyond the establishment of English-immigrant villages and towns, to the reorganisation of the landscape itself. Some densely settled unfree Welsh communities on the broadest lowland coastal plains of Wales were no doubt incorporated with little change into newly imposed Anglo-Norman administrative structures (see below). But most free and many unfree *gwelyau*, as territorial or simply familial units, were characterised by non-nucleated settlement. Here, isolated farmsteads were distributed around the fringes of the arable landscape – that is, the old *tir cyfrif* shareland – in a 'girdle pattern', so that individual farmers might move easily between crops on lowland arable and cattle in upland pastures.[34] Representative of this girdle pattern is the north Pembrokeshire medieval Welsh community of Mynachlog-ddu.[35] In contrast, incoming English settlers lived next door to one another in nucleated settlements from which peasant labourers walked to the surrounding common fields worked by the village community as a whole. Modern satellite imagery lays bare just how starkly these alternative agricultural regimes differed. For example, one can compare the isolated farmsteads of Mynachlog-ddu to the Anglicised south Pembrokeshire village of Manorbier, from which hailed the famed mixed-heritage churchman and author Gerald of Wales. To this day, Manorbier comprises a dense cluster of houses flanked by a castle, medieval parish church and long narrow fields of amalgamated medieval 'strips', or peasant shares of the common fields, possibly comprising a Norman repurposing of prehistoric linear features.[36]

Following the example of William fitz Osbern's 1067 invasion of Gwent, generations of Norman lords and their fighting men conquered manageable parcels of the Welsh landscape, which came to be called 'marcher lordships'. Over these, they exercised almost complete authority, made durable through the construction of castles. They imported English peasant cultivators, often of unfree status, to till the best lowland arable and to produce agricultural surpluses for market (see below), and they established trading settlements, such as Monmouth and Chepstow, for the support and auxiliary defence of their outposts.

Demographic change to c.1100

Welsh social and economic structures were not static in the centuries before the arrival of the Normans in 1067 and the extension of their power into particular localities thereafter. This is illustrated by the emergence of semi-free and free *gwelyau*, as discussed above. It is difficult to know with certainty by what point in time a native socioeconomic configuration dominated by semi-free and free *gwelyau*, most with only small arable shares, had arisen, but Jones Pierce and Glanville Jones both argued that c.1100 was a turning point.[37] That is to say, Welsh freemen were already, out of necessity, settling in the early twelfth century what historians of England would call 'marginal' lands, a century or more before English peasants in most areas would be forced to do the same.[38] Anglo-Norman colonisation only exacerbated the problem (see below). As Ian Jack wrote, 'Virtually all the good land was occupied early, especially by the Norman conquerors of the south and east in the eleventh and twelfth century. All response to population or other pressures therefore was into marginal land.'[39] Mark Bailey has argued of England that areas only marginally suitable for arable agriculture could be exploited through pastoral agriculture to produce dairy, hides and wool that could be exchanged for foodstuffs, making life on marginal lands tenable, while specialisation of production and even the sale of surplus labour could enhance the viability of life at the margin.[40] But this required a market economy, for which there is little evidence in most of Wales before the thirteenth century, and a sufficient density of population in adjacent areas to consume the specialised upland products and to offer opportunities to sell one's labour, which did not exist in Wales (see below, 'The impact of rural colonisation').

Economic and social change in the period after 1100 has been surveyed by Antony Carr. Lacking demographic data from Wales, he reflected on the developed historiography of medieval England where population may have as much as tripled between 1066 and 1500, and asserted that, as in England, 'the primary cause of economic change in Wales was the rise in population, the result of a period of favourable climate between 1050 and 1300'.[41] But the supposition that substantial twelfth- and thirteenth-century population growth happened in Wales, accelerating a trend already under way before 1100, is problematic. It is based on the incorrect assumption that English evidence can speak for Wales, and hinges on the continued availability and growing exploitation of substantial quantities of previously unutilised or under-utilised arable farmland. Wales, in the twelfth century, simply lacked a reserve of arable land equivalent to that of England. An assessment of the development of Welsh agriculture to about 1100 illustrates this point.

Acute native population pressure on resources may have been a significant factor in Wales well before 1100. Wendy Davies has identified more than half a dozen famines in late tenth-century Wales; she has pointed out that medieval famine might equally be caused by a lack of manpower to exploit the available resources or insufficient resources when fully exploited to feed the population.[42] Bad weather could also cause famine. But Davies has acknowledged that the eleventh-century story of King Meirchion criticizes preserving lands for hunting that might be better turned over to cultivation, suggesting a social consciousness of land shortage by the time of the Norman invasion.[43]

Comparison of lands conveyed in seventh- to eleventh-century charters of the bishops of the Welsh diocese of Llandaff and the English diocese of Worcester, on opposing sides of the Severn, has indicated that 'There is a clear and direct link between the size and quality of estates held by Llandaff: estates of good quality tend to be smaller in size with the estate's size increasing as quality deteriorates . . . This link does not, however, appear in those estates owned by Worcester.'[44] Christopher Hurley, finding the reason for this 'unclear', notes that Worcester lands were more aggressively managed and speculates that greater manpower, strictly directed, may have better manipulated natural resources through drainage, manuring and crop management to raise the soils beyond their natural potential.[45] A more straightforward explanation is that donors to Llandaff, wishing to make a substantial gift, were already forced to offset a lack of fertile arable with the gift of larger areas of less valuable upland; this implies that non-arable upland pursuits generated much less income than lowland arable agriculture. Pastoral agriculture produces less than one-fifth the calories per acre of arable agriculture (see below). The inescapable reality is that 58 per cent of Wales lies at an elevation of 500 feet or more above sea level, beyond which contemporary arable agriculture was tenuous or impossible – compared to considerably less than 33 per cent of Worcester Cathedral properties – and many rocky or boggy lowlands too are unsuitable for cultivation.[46] This severely limited the scope for human effort to increase medieval agricultural production in Wales and, in turn, for population and economic output to grow. By the twelfth century, under the prevailing socioeconomic regime, there was little scope for growth, and there is no evidence of a trajectory of strong growth before the twelfth century. Surveys of preserved pollens, while still very few for Wales, have shown no discernible increase in the proportion of land used for arable farming across the period AD 43–1066, while parallel work on the bordering western lowlands of England have suggested a 33–50 per cent increase.[47] Even by modern reckoning, only 14 per cent, or $c.$610,000 acres, of modern Wales is 'croppable', probably not vastly more than was available to Welsh cultivators of the same area in 1066.[48]

In sharp contrast, in 1100 England still had room to expand its population and arable output. Twelfth-century England is understood to have experienced an unparalleled expansion and enhancement of agriculture, particularly the 'colonisation', or cultivation, of previously unexploited lands suitable or made suitable for arable agriculture.[49] This, in turn, fuelled unprecedented demographic and economic growth. It is now understood that the amount of arable land made ready for cultivation in England doubled between 1086 – as recorded in the Domesday survey – and 1290, from $c.$6 million acres to $c.$12 million acres, in conjunction with as much as a trebling of the population from around two million to around six million.[50] Meanwhile, less productive, if less labour-intensive, pastoral agriculture was displaced from cultivable land, and its relative importance to the economy reached an historic low as medieval English population peaked in the decades before the Black Death of 1348–9.[51] This was a pragmatic response to the needs of the rapidly growing population. The difference in energy yield per acre, between cattle and wheat, the preferred cereal for the medieval market, is staggering. Accepting that all agricultural output is necessarily variable, as a mid-twentieth-century frame of reference, beef cattle then produced about 304 Mcal (1 Megacalorie = 1,000,000 calories) per acre, and dairy cattle produced about 1,012 Mcal per acre, while wheat produced about 5,668 Mcal per acre.[52] That is to say, arable agriculture produces 5.6 times as much energy per acre as dairy cattle and 18.6 times as much energy as beef cattle. While these forms of agriculture, not yet mechanised, were self-evidently not equally efficient in terms of the energy expenditure required of the farmer, the simple truth that more food could be produced per acre through arable farming was well understood by medieval people, driving the expansion of arable farming as population grew. In turn, this provided more scope for demographic and economic growth. Stephen Broadberry, Bruce Campbell, et al. have argued that increasing population density can also result in the opening up of new uplands for animal husbandry, producing dairy, meat, hides and wool, with higher population density driving perceptibly higher pastoral yields.[53] But any potential for growth and profitability in upland pastoral communities required that sufficient and affordable arable surpluses, especially grain, be available in exchange for pastoral produce, and that reliable venues for that exchange, such as regular markets, should exist. While these conditions were emergent in England by 1100, only from the thirteenth century would they be present in much of Wales, with the development of urban trade networks (see below).

Throughout the bulk of predominantly upland Wales, extensive expansion of genuinely productive arable was not possible. Much of the agricultural expansion that did take place was achieved by temporary outfield cultivation, and the earliest Welsh law texts, compiled by the early twelfth century, already distinguish between productive *erwau* (arable acres) and ploughed furrows, elsewhere called 'mountain land'.[54] This latter land came to cover several times as great an area as the *erwau*, but could only be cultivated at long intervals.[55]

Population increase was constrained by the lower agricultural productivity of the pastoral upland districts into which growing *gwelyau* expanded from at least 1100, and secondarily by recurrent warfare between the minor kingdoms of Wales in competition for the country's limited resources.[56] Thus Wales may have been reaching its arable-maximum precisely when England was beginning a century or more of agricultural, demographic and economic expansion. The difference in scope for arable expansion between Wales and England was crucial, for as Finbar McCormick has succinctly written of predominately upland, pastoral economies, after analysing the analogous situation in contemporary Ireland:

> 'Such systems . . . do not allow economic development because dairy produce does not easily lend itself to the production and accumulation of significant surplus nor is dairy produce particularly suitable for economic expansion based on trade. Its perishable nature militates against both roles. To develop political power that is based on economic power and wealth it is necessary to change the emphasis from livestock to cereal production.'[57]

There is every reason to believe that native Wales may well have fallen into the 'Malthusian trap' of naturally exponential population growth butting up against modest arithmetic increases in food production as early as the period around 1100. By this date, Welsh society was chronically near the margin of subsistence and was able to expand only into upland areas suitable for pastoral agriculture and intermittent unproductive cultivation, while lacking the market economy necessary to exchange efficiently inedible upland products (for example, hides and wool) for lowland grain. As a result, it was locked into what Colin Thomas has called a 'closed system'. That is 'in the sense that while it had to meet external obligations such as taxes, the resources available [to any one *gwely*] were circumscribed by jealously protected boundaries with other similar communities, by technological deficiencies and traditional agricultural practices' while, 'by the early thirteenth century [*if not before*] there was no unfettered colonisation frontier'.

The agrarian economy before the Black Death

The primary cause of economic change in Wales after 1100 was not a sharp rise in the native population, but instead the impact of the external forces of Norman and English political conquest, and immigration from a demographically ascendant England (see below). William Rees, one of a small group of enterprising early twentieth-century historians who first turned their hands to the economic history of Wales, in 1924 set out the 'economic organization of the lordships of Wales' created by William fitz Osbern and the conquerors who would follow him as comprising three elements.[59] The elements are 'the castle', 'the manor' – referred to by modern scholars as the 'Englishry' – and 'the Welsh lands: the Welshry'.[60] These divisions continue to provide a useful intellectual schema, to which we need add only the oft-neglected topic of the town in Wales, which is addressed separately below. They represent an administrative colonisation that would accompany and facilitate the rural colonisation of Wales by English peasant colonists.

The 'castle', as both a structure and administrative concept, represents the authority, rights and economic power of the lord. Norman and English lords of lands in Wales, called 'marcher' lords because the 'March' they ruled over comprised territory neither in England nor in *pura Wallia* (that is, native-controlled 'pure Wales'), held most of the revenue-generating powers of the English kings, and exercised those powers with fewer checks on their authority.[61] The castle housed the lord's officials, including a treasurer or 'receiver', who collected moneys from fines levied on commercial exchanges and property transfers, from perquisites of the courts, from the 'farming', or leasing, of lordship assets (e.g. mills and fish weirs) and offices (e.g. forester and *amobrer*), and from rents and dues paid by the tenantry. He also discharged moneys for the maintenance of structures, payment of soldiers and other costs. Large lordships, such as Glamorgan, even had a lordship 'exchequer', in imitation of the office of the exchequer of the English Crown, which received and discharged royal funds.[62]

The 'manor', or 'Englishry', was all or a part of the lordship that had been militarily subjugated and economically reoriented towards the production of surpluses, particularly in grain (preferably in wheat), which might be extracted as annual rents or occasional fines in kind or cash for the profit of the lord. Rees preferred the term 'manor' seemingly because – seduced by Seebohm's incorrect depiction of Wales as semi-nomadic and tribal – there was no greater contrast than between the decentralised Welsh mode of production on scattered farmsteads, as at Mynachlog-ddu, and the stereotyped nucleated English village of so-called 'champion England', as aped at Manorbier (see above). Champion England, a broad swathe of the most fertile farmland of England, stretching from Wiltshire in the south-west to Yorkshire in the northeast, was dominated by large manors populated in the main by unfree tenants who cultivated two or three large open fields, and owed heavy labour services to their lord, working the lord's demesne lands, carrying mill stones, repairing structures and other tasks.[63] Manors of this kind, with a manor house and nucleated peasant village, were all but unknown in Wales c.1066. However, Norman and English invaders created manors in their wake from lands confiscated, or 'escheated', from those who fought against their annexation of Welsh territory or died without heirs. In doing so, they focused their efforts overwhelmingly on the lowland coastal plain and river valleys most suitable for the growing of grain. They populated manor lands with a combination of surviving Welsh and new English tenants, both unfree and free. Collectively, the lands converted to manors and otherwise dominated by English tenants comprised the 'Englishry'.

In some lordships, such as the small lordship of Radnor on the English border, the landscape was divided administratively between a lowland 'Englishry' formed from conquered and escheated lands used mainly for grain production, and a primarily upland 'Welshry', orientated towards pastoral agriculture. In Rees's words, 'rents and services characterised the one and tribute the other'; rents and services were financial and labour obligations dictated by one's personal status that tied people to the lord whose land they cultivated; tribute was a communal payment in recognition of the military supremacy of the lord over the lands the community occupied.[54] Rees suspected that the 'primarily economic' distinction between the two regions led to the hardening of separate judicial units, but the story is probably more complex. Pre-conquest Welsh *gwelyau* often practised transhumance over lands spread over upland and lowland zones. Norman invasions disturbed these complex units. Unfortunately, we have little evidence for the early Welsh arable economy in many southern and eastern parts of Wales, as documentary record keeping would only come about after Norman dominance. This is especially true with respect to the remnants of Welsh unfree communities that historically cultivated *tir cyfrif*, or shareland. From the twelfth century, these groups were either recast as free *gwelyau*, as in Cardiganshire, or simply amalgamated with unfree English settlers into the bond communities that cultivated Anglo-Norman demesne lands.[65] On Anglesey, for example, among areas that remained longest under native control, early post-conquest records, such as the lay subsidy returns of 1292–3, suggest both the great importance of arable agriculture and the economic significance of *maerdref* demesne lands on which unfree tenants were bound to do agricultural day works.[66]

The third element of Rees's schema was 'the Welsh lands: the Welshry'. This was that part of the country, nominally under Anglo-Norman control, where resided the bulk of the Welsh population, continuing to live largely by Welsh law and to hold many lands by the common ownership of the *gwely*. Importantly, while a formal administrative distinction between an Englishry and a Welshry did not exist in all lordships, most maintained a *de facto* segregation.[67] In south Wales, in particular, Welshries were ethnic communities focused on the upland remainders of old Welsh territorial units conquered by incoming Norman lords. For instance, the medieval lordship of Ogmore was a sub-lordship of the lordship of Glamorgan, which was itself roughly analogous to the western half of the old Welsh kingdom of Morgannwg, and loosely equated to the earlier post-Roman kingdom of Glywysing, which spanned upland and lowland zones. Yet the twelfth-century and later Englishry of southern Ogmore comprised the fertile soils that would make the lowland 'Vale of Glamorgan' famous for its agriculture, while Welsh Ogmore contained extensive pasture land and forests shot through with bleak mountains and high peaks, earning it the name 'Ogmore in the wood'.[68] Such Welshries persevered, for some centuries, *gwelyau* structures, together with Welsh law and custom. But the *longue durée* of upland Welsh land holding tells the story of the collapse of the *gwely* system of agricultural production. In the first half of the fourteenth century many of the hillsides in the Welshries were more densely populated than they are in the early twenty-first century.[70] As Margaret Davies observed, at an early stage, the people of the Welshries paid their communal 'tribute' in kind from the produce of small arable plots and much larger common pastures, but by the fifteenth century enclosed upland arable fields, farmed in severalty, for which individual tenants paid cash rents, were more typical.[71] This removed the need for the cooperation of the *gwely*, undermining what was probably its prime *raison d'être*.

The impact of rural colonisation, 1067–1315

The 'closed system' of the Welsh agricultural economy as described by Thomas, with little scope for internal growth, was opened violently to change by Norman and English invaders.[72] Invasion, leading to the creation of a bifurcated society of predominately lowland Englishries and upland Welshries, permitted economic expansion. The political power of the Englishry was based on cereal production, while the Welsh population and the remainder of its political community was relegated by incoming post-conquest English settlers to largely pastoral upland districts. There, on thin soils, they strained sourly against the limits of agriculture, lacking scope to move beyond an inefficient pastoral economy until the integration of Welsh upland production with newly established lowland-based market economies, the eventual breakdown of the *gwely* system and ultimately the abolition of ethnic segregation following the Act of Union of 1536.

Wales, unlike England, did not experience radical demographic and economic growth between 1100 and 1300 as a result of the expansion of arable output, but experienced only modest growth as a result of the attempted cultivation of upland 'marginal' land, and substantial English immigration that stimulated cereal- and market-based economic development.[73] Understanding the balance between these two latter causes of demographic growth is crucial to the historian but is difficult to establish because quantifiable demographic evidence survives only from the late thirteenth century onwards. By this date, the population of Wales was already at its maximum observable medieval level, of 250,000–300,000 people

Rees Davies grappled with this lack of evidence in the 1980s, writing that pre-conquest population trends can 'hardly be broached', but that 'undoubted population increase . . . in the twelfth and thirteenth centuries . . . was fed from two sources: from a marked growth of population in native society and from very considerable alien immigration into south and east Wales.'[74] Davies's conjecture that 'marked growth' took place in native society post 1100 was based on the high population densities observable in the late thirteenth-century villages of upland Merionethshire, but this evidence is problematic.[75] There is little to indicate the novelty of these upland communities nor the scale of population increase they show in a mountainous district where demographic pressure on arable lands likely arose at a much earlier stage than in England (as argued above); Davies simply assumed that these impressionistic data were a parallel with the well-documented process of agricultural and demographic expansion found in twelfth- and thirteenth-century England. A more appropriate context for understanding the Merionethshire evidence may be provided by Jones's analysis of medieval settlement distribution in Anglesey, which found that new free townships emerging from the mid-eleventh century were located overwhelmingly on 'relatively infertile' lands. Thus, by the time of the composition of late thirteenth-century royal surveys, 26 per cent of the island's 200 vills and hamlets lay on 'shallow drought-prone soils' (3 per cent) or soils with 'seasonally or permanently impeded drainage' (23 per cent).[76] As a very crude measure of population increase, the foundation of these additional villages on marginal soils suggest population growth of about 35 per cent between *c.*1050 and *c.*1300, or, if generously doubled to account for increased population density within pre-existing villages, 70 per cent; not as much as the 200 per cent population increase experienced in England.[77]

Wales was not without some notable efforts at arable land reclamation, the most substantial of which was probably the 27,000 acres or so of reclaimed estuarine alluvium known as the 'Gwent Levels' along the Welsh shore of the Severn Sea between Cardiff and Chepstow, exploited progressively from the early twelfth century.[78] However, this area was the first in all Wales subject to Anglo-Norman control – from the late eleventh century. It saw extensive English immigration, and it was heavily manorialised, including highly regulated bond communities (as at Caldicot, discussed in Chapter 3). In short, largely low-lying Gwent was atypical of Wales, and was colonised in every sense by the English.[79]

Immigration to Wales was at least as important to demographic change as was growth within native communities, but the initial arrival of Anglo-Norman invaders from 1067 in Gwent, and throughout Wales thereafter, may sometimes have had a neutral or even negative impact on population density.[80] The range of late medieval English place names from across the forming Englishries of South and East Wales – such as Carew Newtown, New House, New Moat (Pembroke); New Nottage (Glamorgan); or New Radnor (Radnorshire) reflect the establishment of immigrant communities.[81] The process of rural colonisation was extremely diverse, echoing the pace of Anglo-Norman conquest and the differing whims of local lords with respect to how best to recruit colonists and where to install them for maximum profitable effect. For example, in Gwent, morphological studies of settlements indicate that the early Norman conquest did not lead to the foundation of new villages on existing arable and that the late medieval tenants of the sub-lordship of Caldicot were overwhelmingly English, which suggests the displacement of prior Welsh tenants and their replacement with English incomers.[82] The English names of villages on the adjoining but reclaimed lands of the Gwent Levels, such as Redwick and Whitson, do suggest English immigration or at least land colonisation that simply supplemented the lordship's population.[83] Nevertheless, Gwent was atypical as a marcher lordship in which there was scope for substantial land reclamation.

Thus, rather than immigration supplementing rural Welsh population (see below for urban immigration), English immigration to the Welsh countryside was characterised by the displacement of the native Welsh population from lowland to upland areas and its replacement with immigrant tenants. Bookending the long 'Age of Conquest' of Wales are Henry I's implantation of a Flemish community in the vicinity of Haverfordwest (Pembrokeshire) in 1107–10 and the Earl of Lincoln, Henry de Lacy's creation of an English colony in his new lordship of Denbigh (Denbighshire), from 1284. At Haverfordwest, Flemings arrived at the Crown's invitation in the hope of establishing a local cloth industry. They were both preceded and followed by substantial English immigration, leading to the creation of a band of planned and partially planned villages across the Pembrokeshire 'Landsker line' that continue to comprise the Anglo-Welsh linguistic frontier, testifying to the ambition and scale of immigration.[84] Lowland Pembrokeshire, by 1290, was the most densely populated part of Wales, with around 103 persons per square mile, more than double that of the less fertile and overwhelmingly native north Pembrokeshire cantref of Pebidiog.[85] Southern Pembrokeshire has historically been, and continues to be, colloquially referred to as 'Little England beyond Wales', and recent DNA analysis has highlighted the 'stark differences' between the genetic profiles of the inhabitants of the predominantly upland pastoral north and the predominately lowland arable south of the county.[86] All of this suggests that immigration displaced and replaced the Welsh population. Such indirect evidence is not required to see Earl de Lacy's implantation of an English colony in Denbighshire, over a century and a half later, as he created a 'cohesive English colony' based on good arable appropriated through escheat or exchange, amounting to some thousands of acres. This can be observed in a detailed lordship survey of 1334.[87]

With respect to both the lordships of Pembroke and Denbigh, it is reasonable to ask whether the displaced Welsh could readily have been fed and supported by the uplands to which they relocated. In the 1190s Gerald of Wales described the great fertility of Anglesey, 'able to supply all of Wales', by contrasting it with the poor 'natural fertility' of Pebidiog.[88] Given the lower productivity of both upland soils and pastoral agriculture – at least five times *less* productive than arable in terms of calorie output, as discussed above – short- to medium-term population loss would have been inevitable. The, at least initial, hardship and extreme poverty caused by this dislocation was no doubt a 'push factor' behind the otherwise surprising willingness of Welshmen to serve in marcher and royal armies hard on the heels of Anglo-Welsh conflict. As Rees Davies acknowledged, even as early as 1169 'population pressure was such that native Welsh peasants and Anglo-Norman settlers alike were attracted in considerable numbers to take part in the colonisation of Ireland' – an expedition that departed from Pembroke.[89] More remarkable still is the extraordinary total of 19,500 Welshmen who served as the king's soldiers in Wales in 1287, and 10,900 who served at Falkirk, Scotland, in 1298; the number of Welshmen in royal armies declined thereafter.[90] The Welsh contingents of these latter armies, raised shortly after the conquest and confiscations of 1282–4 and the national rebellion of 1294–5 would then have comprised about 26 per cent and 15 per cent, respectively, of the adult male population of *c.*75,000.[91] More still would have followed in the baggage train, and many would never have returned, resulting in native depopulation.

It is nevertheless possible, and even likely, that English immigration resulted in a net population increase across the twelfth and thirteenth centauries, if still far less than the trebling of population that occurred in England. The scale of rural immigration, especially to those parts of Wales that saw the violent expulsion of existing Welsh communities, must have been at least commensurate to the scale of Welsh displacement. Free settlers, especially those granted more sizeable estates, were typically required to render castle-guard duty well into the thirteenth century or beyond, a century after the custom's decline and commutation to a cash payment in England.[92]

The density of rural English immigrant settlement in Wales varied widely, and is first observable in documentation from the early thirteenth century. In the post-conquest Principality, despite earlier periodic English domination, immigration was limited almost entirely to urban centres. For example, the area that comprised the northern component of the Welsh kingdom of Deheubarth, later designated Cardiganshire, was first invaded in 1093, but by *c*.1300 English settler families comprised only about one-in-fifteen of an approximate population of 10,000 and lived almost exclusively within the franchises of Cardigan and Llanbadarn (that is, Aberystwyth).[93] In the March, by contrast, immigration was much more substantial, as is suggested by the distinct linguistic and genetic footprint it has left in south Pembrokeshire, discussed above. Property-holder and taxpayer-name data *c*.1300, even when excluding predominantly English urban populations (see below), suggest that 7 per cent of Flintshire inhabitants were English, as were 10 per cent of inhabitants of the mid-March old counties of Radnor and Brecon and 17 per cent of inhabitants of northern and eastern Gwent.[94] Naturally the density of rural immigrant settlement *c*.1300 was much higher in any given 'Englishry', as in the lordship of Dyffryn Clwyd (Denbighshire), colonised from 1280s, where 32 per cent of free tenants (24 per cent of all tenants) of the commote of Llannerch were identified as 'English', or Radnor Englishry, colonised from the 1090s, where 47 per cent of taxpayers had English names.[95] The degree of immigration these data suggest would have been sorely felt by the Welsh communities whose lands were expropriated, typically from among the best arable acres, but it would not have been sufficient to augment radically the total population – at least on the scale of growth experienced in contemporary England.

It is possible that the impact of immigration on agricultural output was greater than immigrant numbers might suggest. An important plank of the story of rapid population growth in England, in addition to the doubling of arable under cultivation, is the introduction of new farming technologies, especially the three-field system in preference to the native reliance on two-field systems. In two-field systems the land was partitioned roughly equally each year between fallow and crop, field usage alternating from year to year. In three-field systems, the land was partitioned into three parts, with one part left fallow, one part planted with a winter cereal crop, such as wheat, and one part planted with a spring cereal crop such as oats or barley.[96] The two crops were then 'rotated' though the three fields sequentially. From the fourteenth century, this system was increasingly enhanced by the introduction of a restorative nitrogen-fixing legume crop – namely peas, vetches or beans

– into the rotation.⁹⁷ Three-field systems could, at least in the short term, increase total food output because more of the total arable was cropped annually. And, because it entailed harvests of two different crops each year instead of one, it mitigated the risk of total crop failure and famine. Three-field technology was progressively adopted in the latter part of the period of English immigration to Wales, *c.*1067–1300. Nevertheless, the impact of such technologies on total food output, and by extension demographic and economic growth in Wales, must have been muted at best. As mentioned above, even by modern reckoning no more than 14 per cent of Wales is 'croppable', less still in the Middle Ages.⁹⁸ Jack's extensive survey of field systems in Wales before 1350 found evidence of open-field agriculture, particularly in the mid-March and across the south Wales coastal belt of good arable below 500 to 600 feet.⁹⁹ He found occasional evidence of three-field systems employing three-course crop rotation scattered throughout the English borderlands and south Wales along with scattered evidence of both two-course crop rotation and infield-outfield agriculture, the 'outfields' being less productive fields occasionally sown. The relative antiquity of these regimes, three-field systems being of the greatest interest, is impossible to gauge from the mostly post-1290 evidence of their existence. Two main points, however, are discernible from Jack's work. On the one hand, three-field systems *c.*1300 were most prevalent in the March, especially areas of more substantial English immigration. Immigrants tending to have colonised the most fertile lands of Wales, this offers some support to the contested assertion made by Howard Gray, over a century ago, that three-field systems are best associated with richer soils and two-field systems with poorer soils.¹⁰⁰ On the other hand, three-field agriculture was by no means demonstrably a staple of, or exclusive to, English settler agriculture, coexisting and evolving alongside other agricultural regimes in both England and Wales, as it did in Pembrokeshire alongside infield-outfield agriculture.¹⁰¹

Moreover, even where three-field agriculture was practised, it may not necessarily have achieved substantially greater productivity than two-field systems. While yields per seed planted were relatively high on some well-documented manors where three-field rotational systems were employed, as at Cuxham (Oxfordshire), Campbell has demonstrated that dense seeding and intensive cultivation leaving little annual fallow could drive up productivity impressively under two-field and infield-outfield arable regimes – the systems employed by the native Welsh.[102] Besides, any technological advantage enjoyed by incoming English settlers would have been put to the test simply to produce grain yields in Wales approaching those they achieved back in England. A variety of factors, including an overabundance of marginal soils and high levels of precipitation, resulted in a preference for oat cultivation over wheat cultivation and generally poorer yields per seed planted in the southern and eastern March of Wales than are observable in the English borderlands (see below).

While wheat was the most valued medieval market crop for human consumption – wheat, by volume, typically selling for at least 150 per cent the price of oats – the population of Wales grew and ate substantially more oats (the staple element of the Welsh diet was the oat-cake), which are more tolerant of high rainfall and poor soils.[103] Surviving elements of the 1284 post-conquest royal extent of Gwynedd show the populace to be in possession of five times as much oats as wheat.[104] In the court rolls of fourteenth-century Dyffryn Clwyd, which include inventories, thefts, debts and other transactions, wheat is found in only small quantities of two to four bushels, while oats were typically recorded in quarters or more (1 quarter = 8 bushels).[105] Probate inventory evidence of mid-sixteenth- to mid-seventeenth- century West Glamorgan (previously the lordship of Gower) have shown that, even in the best lowland soils, oats and wheat were grown on roughly equal acreages and that even here some farmers planted two or three times as many acres in oats as in wheat.[106] In this way, the March was a hybrid economy, situated between the post-conquest Principality, where vastly more oats than wheat were grown –sometimes to the complete exclusion of wheat – and the English borderlands of Herefordshire, where wheat dominated all other crops, often by more than two to one.[107] Moreover, given the greater value of wheat, this conveys something of the hierarchy of arable economic output, lowest in Welsh Wales and highest in England, with the March somewhere in between.

With respect to yields, typical medieval yields in neighbouring lowland England were 5 units harvested per unit of seed sown (that is, 5:1) for wheat, 8:1 for barley and 4:1 for oats.[108] Yield data from Wales are scarce, but some are available. Wheat yields recorded in 1326 on the bishop of St David's estates in Brecknock, Cardigan, Glamorgan and Pembroke indicate yields of just 3:1 to 4:1.[109] Monmouthshire may have performed better, with wheat yields on scattered Clare family holdings in 1329 and 1339 averaging about 5:1, which was similar to the mean yields of Herefordshire and Shropshire estates in the 1320s. Oat yields, of greater importance to subsistence, were similarly poor in Wales. On the bishop's estates, in 1326, they averaged only about 2.5:1, while in Monmouthshire, 1329 and 1339, the average was about 3.5:1.[110] In contrast to their substantially better-than-Wales wheat yields, Herefordshire and Shropshire had below-English-average oat yields in the late thirteenth and early fourteenth century (excluding famine years), typically about 3:1.[111] But it may be that in these mainly wheat-growing English borderlands oats were sown in poorer marginal soils. Ultimately, based on these yields, lowland Glamorgan, known within medieval and early modern Wales for its productivity, was probably of little more than average fertility by English standards.

What then of upland productivity? Could a radical increase in upland pastoral productivity over the two and a half centuries after the first arrival of Norman invaders have fuelled population increase and economic growth? In short, no. There are two reasons for this.

As Thomas has argued, even in upland areas of Wales 'tillage' and 'pastoralism' are artificial divisions imposed by modern misinterpretation of what was an integrated economy in which no more than a quarter of families were pastoralists entirely dependent on dairy, meat and other animal products, who grew no crops at all.[112] Individual peasant families in predominantly upland Wales, whether bond or free, did not have a great deal more livestock than peasant families in England, with its vast tracts of arable. Surviving elements of the 1284 post-conquest royal extent of Gwynedd, covering 361 families, indicate that the 'typical' or *median* family had three head of cattle (e.g. cows and heifers), two oxen, a horse and five sheep, with pastoral activities providing two-thirds of familial wealth.[113] The relative numbers of sheep and cattle varied in accordance with the quality of graze available to the family, cattle requiring better grasses. By comparison, Philip Slavin's recent survey of nearly 4,000 English peasant inventories (including a small amount of Monmouthshire data) found the *mean* peasant family to have two head of cattle, every third family to have an ox and slightly fewer to have a horse.[114] Similarly Postan's research on southern and eastern England suggested that the *mean* family had ten or fewer sheep, though in reality sheep were clustered into few hands, and rearing them was something of a 'rich man's occupation'.[115] Based on analysis of a selection of Suffolk and Wiltshire 'arable' and 'pastoral' locations, Postan found a 'functional insufficiency' of livestock (i.e. insufficient to produce needed manure for arable fields), with pastoral activities providing just 55 per cent and 44 per cent of familial wealth in 'pastoral' and 'arable' villages, respectively – the distinction between village types here too acknowledged as 'something of a phantom', as virtually all communities grew some crops and had some livestock.[116] Nevertheless, these English families, with their collective 'insufficiency' of livestock and a relative abundance of cultivatable land– had nearly half as much livestock as Welsh peasant families in a region where less than 14 per cent of the land was croppable and people were overwhelmingly dependent for survival on pastoral production.[117] The net result contributed to the relative poverty of Wales compared to England, *c*.1290, as suggested by the per capita wealth of the Church in Wales – itself derived overwhelmingly from tithes and agricultural production – at 4.2 pence, versus England, at 7.7 pence (see below, Chapter 2).[118]

Commutation and urbanisation

The shift from a society based on payments in kind to one in which money dominated transactions (initially money of account and later in specie) transformed the economy of Wales. It was made possible by the introduction of towns, an element largely neglected by Rees and additional to his own tripartite schema of 'castle', 'manor' (that is, Englishry) and 'Welshry' discussed above. In fact, Rees's understatement of the importance of early towns would be echoed by historians of Wales for over forty years, with Lynn Nelson commenting in his seminal 1966 work, *The Normans in South Wales*, that boroughs 'of the Welsh frontier were an artificial growth, stimulated by the needs of a garrison society ... merely extensions of the castles near which they were built'.[119] This view overlooks the importance of towns, not just in stimulating taxable bulk and retail trade, as settlements such as Carmarthen or Chepstow would by the fourteenth century, but also in creating what Jim Bolton has called 'a monetised economy' reckoning monetary values for peasant taxation and administration, as a precursor of commercialisation.[120]

Anglo-Normans facilitated 'commutation' in much of Wales, that is to say, the conversion of labour services and other dues into cash payments. The Welsh did not mint coins, but coin-hungry early Norman invaders invited moneyers to mint English *Paxis* type coins, 1087–*c*.1100, at Cardiff, St David's, Abergavenny and Rhuddlan, with Cardiff and new mints at Swansea and Pembroke active *c*.1100–1158 (coins, as pictured throughout this volume).[121] The value of money, both the innate worth of the silver that was used to produce pennies – the near-universal form of medieval coinage – and its utility in simplifying and lubricating exchange and commerce, were understood by Welsh rulers. Coin finds suggest that Roman specie had circulated freely in the land, in south Wales in particular.[122] But the steady supplies of silver and political stability necessary for the operation of a mint eluded the Welsh princes, who relied on foreign coins for external payments. Welsh rulers collected dues and services in kind, until at least the thirteenth century, when fledgling attempts were made by the princes of Gwynedd to ascribe monetary values to the dues and services rendered by their own tenants, and possibly even to collect them in English coin where achievable (as opposed to reckoning the cash values of goods offered against cash values of dues and services owed).[123]

As indicated above, military-commercial town plantation was central to the pattern of sustainable Norman conquest and control, even from William fitz Osbern's first foray into Gwent and his foundation of the fortified sites that would become Monmouth and Chepstow in 1067. The first academic research on the small towns of Wales was pioneered by Edward Lewis, an older contemporary of William Rees, who focused on the final phase of town foundation in Wales, that initiated by Edward I following his 'final conquest' of *pura Wallia* in 1282–4, over two hundred years after fitz Osbern's first invasion.[124] Lewis published his path-breaking study of *The Medieval Boroughs of Snowdonia* in 1912, looking at Edward's deliberate creation of planned boroughs for the benefit of incoming English colonists entering the former heartlands of the deposed Prince Llywelyn ap Gruffydd as an expression of concerted political and commercial effort.[125] Lewis rightly saw these towns as an attempt to harness the 'rustic Welsh' to the cart of the 'mercantile English' drivers of the commercialising economy, and, more importantly, to concentrate trade in formally constituted towns within prescribed market districts.[126] Lewis described Edwardian ordinances that gave urban property owners a range of freedoms from toll and low fixed rents, while fining any Welsh caught trading outside Edward's boroughs, as 'transitional links between the old economy and the new'.[127]

Lewis's conclusions regarding Edwardian creations continue to be respected, and were taken forward in the 1960s by Maurice Beresford's *New Towns of the Middle Ages*.[128] But a rising tide of interest in the small towns of medieval Britain, from the late 1970s, has brought to light the commercial and intellectual groundwork laid for Edward I and his advisers by the exertions of over two centuries of lords and traders between fitz Osbern's arrival in Wales and Edward's 'final conquest'. Historians now stress the importance of adopting a functional rather than constitutional definition of what comprised a 'town', in which the focus is on identifying places where most of the population derived most of their income from craft and commerce, that is 'low-level urbanisation'.[129] Most, but not all, such places eventually received a grant of privileges, or 'borough charter', from either the marcher lord, as at Swansea sometime between 1158 and 1184, or, where they were royal possessions, from the English Crown, as at Carmarthen in 1109.[130]

During the first century of town life in Wales (that is, after *c.*1067), this 'institutional urbanism' of privileges recognised and enhanced in borough charters came overwhelmingly *after* the establishment of fledgling trading settlements in the shadows of castles or churches, encouraging what already existed. This was most common in south Wales, where Norman invaders first conquered substantial territories. The usual set of privileges granted to towns in Wales was some version of those granted by fitz Osbern to the city of Hereford sometime before his death in February 1071, for the advantage of immigrating French burgesses.[131] These 'Laws of Hereford', themselves based on the Laws of Breteuil, in Normandy, commonly granted borough property owners rights such as low fixed rents (usually 1s. a year), freedom from tolls, freedom to buy, sell or devise property to heirs, to hold a special town court and even to have an exclusive town trading monopoly over the surrounding farms and villages.[132] These laws, first systematically investigated by Mary Bateson, spread into parts of England, and then throughout Wales and Ireland where they first benefited English immigrants but quickly thereafter benefited anyone buying town property, irrespective of ethnicity.[133]

During the second century of town life in Wales, up to about 1300, the 'institutional urbanism' of privileges was used to inspire commerce and urban life in Wales, either where intended to supplant nearby native settlement or at greenfield sites thought suitable for development.[134] Edward I's creation of a string of new towns in Snowdonia following his victory over Llywelyn ap Gruffydd in 1282, was little more than the climax of what was, by then, a tried, tested and formalised pattern of town foundation. Edward, within a generation, issued charters for more than a dozen prospective boroughs in Wales, including both successful settlements such as Aberystwyth (Cardiganshire, 1277), Rhuddlan (Flintshire, 1278), Conwy (Caernarfonshire, 1283) and Beaumaris (Anglesey, 1295), and unsuccessful settlements such as Castell y Bere (Merionethshire, 1284).

The fostering of commerce where it sprang up, in the first century of town life in Wales after c.1067 – as neglected by Rees, Nelson and Lewis – saw the creation of a monetised economy, in which peasants came to understand the worth of their goods and labour services in terms of cash values. The second century of town life in Wales saw the emergence of what Bolton has called 'a money economy' where

English coins came to circulate with regularity as a preferred means of exchange, and a certain seigniorial mania drove king and lords alike to speculate increasingly on the possibility that a greenfield site granted a charter of generous liberties might, in time, yield a profitable centre of commerce, while reaffirming lordly authority.[135] Lastly, in addition to the encouragement of new towns of mixed military-economic origin, characterised by their function as fortified nodes of English commercial colonisation, ancient points of exchange of purely organic origin, such as Machynlleth (Montgomeryshire), were also reconstituted with privileges.[136]

This rapid urbanisation and commercialisation is attributable, in part, to what Bolton has called a 'flood of silver' entering the economy as the total face value of circulating English coinage (silver pennies, half pennies and farthings), the main coinage to circulate in medieval Wales, increased from as little as £30,000 in the twelfth century to around £2,000,000 by 1319.[137] This coinage flowed into Wales by way of about one hundred new town markets and a similar number of periodic fairs associated with a variety of towns, churches and villages, which played host to local and visiting merchant buyers offering hard cash for agricultural goods.[138] Further, the virtually universal construction of churches and, most importantly, of castles in Wales, overwhelmingly in stone by the thirteenth century, acted as an economic stimulus of unparalleled import. Wales and the Welsh borders remain the most densely castellated area of Europe, and every non-native castle construction required a vast investment of money, raised mostly in England and spent in Wales, on both unskilled local labour and highly skilled artisan labour invited from England. Arnold Taylor has calculated that between 1277 and 1330 Edward I and his successors spent at least £93,346 on building works in Wales, raised from English taxes and loans from Italian bankers. This was a sum equivalent to 5 per cent of all English coinage in existence in 1330, a proportion roughly equivalent to the Welsh population as a part of the combined English and Welsh population (see below).[139] One may add to this extraordinary sum the expenditures of dozens of marcher lords in Wales over two hundred years of occupation, and the cash wages paid to soldiers serving in Wales. Soldiers' pay comprised a substantial part of the remarkable £150,000 expended by Edward on his Welsh campaign of 1282 alone, much of which would have been spent in Wales.[140] Towns were the nodes of commerce through which this flood of silver reached all levels of society in Wales. The first comprehensive survey of medieval Welsh towns, compiled by Ian Soulsby in 1983, identified 105 towns that developed before, after or without ever receiving a charter of institutional privileges. Of these, seventy-five were 'planned alien settlements', although most contained at least a minority Welsh population.[141] When the population of the British Isles reached its medieval peak, c.1300, about 20 per cent of Wales's population of c.250,000 to 300,000 resided in towns, a proportion similar to the town-dwelling sector of English society (see below, Chapter 2, Urbanisation and Immigration).[142] This was an extraordinary economic and social transformation, given that while English urbanism c.1300 was the product of centuries of development, extending back to Roman times and reviving form the tenth century, the urban network of Wales was entirely created in the centuries after fitz Osbern's 1067 invasion.[143]

Notes

1 W. Davies, *Wales in the Early Middle Ages* (Leicester, 1982), pp. 90–112.
2 Welsh: *cantref,* (pl.) *cantrefi*; *cymwd,* (pl.) *cymydau*. No English equivalent exists for *maenor,* (pl.) *maenorau*; sometimes spelled *maenol,* (pl.) *maenolydd*. *Maenor* evolved from the word *mean,* meaning 'stone', rather than the later Anglo-Norman term 'manor' (A. W. Wade-Evans, *Welsh Medieval Law: Being a Text of the Laws of Howel the Good* (Oxford, 1909), p. 344).
3 *AgeCon.,* pp. 136–8.
4 Lord, lordship, Welsh: *arglwydd, arglwyddiaeth,* in *AgeCon.,* p. 137; T. G. Watkin, *The Legal History of Wales,* 2nd edn (Cardiff, 2012), p. 51.

5 *AgeCon.*, pp. 137–8.
6 M. Richards, *Welsh Administrative and Territorial Units: Medieval and Modern* (Cardiff, 1969), p. 233.
7 Richards, *Welsh Administrative and Territorial Units*, p. 250.
8 T. Jones Pierce, 'Pastoral and agricultural settlements in early Wales', in *WelshSoc.*, pp. 347–9; Watkin, *The Legal History*, pp. 51–2.
9 T. Jones Pierce, 'Medieval Cardiganshire – a study in social origins', in *WelshSoc.*, pp. 324–5; Wade-Evans, *Welsh Medieval Law*, p. 344.
10 Jones Pierce, 'Medieval Cardiganshire', pp. 318–19.
11 Jones Pierce, 'Medieval Cardiganshire', pp. 324–5.
12 Jones Pierce, 'Medieval Cardiganshire', p. 315. For a survey of *maerdref* arrangements on Anglesey see A. D. Carr, *Medieval Anglesey*, 2nd edn (Llangefni, 2011), pp. 93–100.
13 Wade-Evans, *Welsh Medieval Law*, p. 345.
14 Carr, *Medieval Anglesey*, pp. 40–1.
15 Carr, *Medieval Anglesey*, p. 41.
16 R. Howell, 'Roman Past and Medieval Present: Caerleon as a Focus for Continuity and Conflict in the Middle Ages', *Studia Celtica*, 46 (2012), 1–21.
17 Much debate surrounds the size, location and nature of 'post-Roman', or 'sub-Roman', points of trade in England and northern Europe. See A. Verhulst, 'The Origins and Early Development of Medieval towns in Northern Europe', *EcHR*, 47 (1994), 362–73.
18 Davies, *Wales in the Early Middle Ages*, pp. 31–58.
19 *AgeCon.*, p. 80.
20 Davies, *Wales in the Early Middle Ages*, pp. 55–6.
21 Davies, *Wales in the Early Middle Ages*, pp. 56–7.
22 Davies, *Wales in the Early Middle Ages*, p. 80.
23 D. Crouch, 'The transformation of medieval Gwent', in *GwentCH*, pp. 1–2.
24 Crouch, 'The transformation of medieval Gwent', pp. 2–3.
25 Jones Pierce, 'Pastoral and agricultural settlements in early Wales', pp. 339–51.
26 T. Jones Pierce, 'Medieval settlement in Anglesey', in *WelshSoc.*, pp. 275–6.
27 Jones Pierce, 'Pastoral and agricultural settlements in early Wales', pp. 341–2.

28 Jones Pierce, 'Medieval Cardiganshire', p. 317.
29 Jones Pierce, 'Medieval Cardiganshire', pp. 309–27.
30 Jones Pierce, 'Medieval Cardiganshire', pp. 318, 322–3.
31 Jones Pierce, 'Medieval Cardiganshire', p. 317.
32 F. A. Seebohm, *The Tribal System in Wales: Being an Inquiry into the Structure and Methods of Tribal Society* (London, 1895).
33 *WelshSoc.*, throughout; G. R. J. Jones, 'The Tribal System in Wales: A Re-assessment in the Light of Settlement Studies', *WHR*, 1 (1960–3), 111–32.
34 Jones, 'The Tribal System', 111–32.
35 J. Howells, 'The countryside', in R. F. Walker (ed.), *Pembrokeshire County History, II: Medieval Pembrokeshire* (Haverfordwest, 2002), pp. 404–6 (*gwelyau*, so called, still existed at nearby Llanfyrnach in 1603, p. 406, n.21).
36 J. Kissock, 'Settlement and society', in *GwentCH*, pp. 70–88.
37 Jones Pierce, 'Pastoral and agricultural settlement in early Wales', pp. 339–51, esp. 341–2; Jones, 'The Tribal System', 131.
38 E. Miller and J. Hatcher, *Medieval England: Rural Society and Economic Change, 1086–1348* (London, 1978), pp. 53–63; critiqued by C. Dyer, *Standards of Living in the Later Middle Ages: Social Change in England, c.1200–1520*, revised edn (Cambridge, 1998), pp. 291–2.
39 R. I. Jack, 'I. Farming techniques: H Wales and the Marches', in H. E. Hallman (ed.), *AgHist.*, II: *1042–1350* (Cambridge, 1988), p. 443.
40 M. Bailey, *A Marginal Economy? East Anglian Breckland in the Later Middle Ages* (Cambridge, 1989), pp. 319–22.
41 A. D. Carr, 'Wales: economy and society', in S. H. Rigby (ed.), *A Companion to Britain in the Later Middle Ages* (Oxford, 2003), p. 126; J. Hatcher and M. Bailey, *Modelling the Middle Ages: The History and Theory of England's Economic Development* (Oxford, 2001), pp. 21–30; see below, Chapter 4.
42 Davies, *Wales in the Early Middle Ages*, pp. 31, 41–2.
43 Davies, *Wales in the Early Middle Ages*, p. 41.
44 C. Hurley, 'Landscapes of Gwent and the Marches as seen through the charters of the seventh to eleventh centuries', in N. Edwards (ed.), *Landscape and Settlement in Medieval Wales* (Oxford, 1997), p. 38.
45 Hurley, 'Landscapes', p. 38.

46 Jack, 'I. Farming techniques', pp. 443.
47 S. Rippon, C. Smart and B. Pears, *The Fields of Britannia: Community and Change in the Late Roman and Early Medieval Landscape* (Oxford, 2015), pp. 252, 299–300.
48 E. Armstrong, 'Research briefing: the farming sector in Wales', *National Assembly for Wales Research Service*, paper 16–053 (2016), 6.
49 Miller and Hatcher, *Medieval England: Rural*, pp. 33–41.
50 Estimates vary; English population was most recently re-estimated by Broadberry et. al as growing from 1.71 million in 1086 to 4.81 million in 1348 (1.71/4.81 = 281%). S. Broadberry, B. M. S. Campbell, A. Klein, M. Overton and B. van Leeuwen, *British Economic Growth, 1270–1870* (Cambridge, 2015), pp. 20–2, 72–3, 114–20 (figures 1.06, 3.04 and tables 3.16–3.19); Hatcher and Bailey, *Modelling the Middle Ages*, p. 29.
51 Broadberry et al., *British Economic Growth*, pp. 114–20 (figure 3.04 and tables 3.16–3.19).
52 W. Holmes, 'The Future of Animals as Sources of Human Food', *Proceedings of the Nutritional Society*, 29 (1970), 241; F. McCormick, 'The Decline of the Cow: Agriculture and Settlement Change in Early Medieval Ireland', *Peritia*, 20 (2008), 219.
53 Broadberry et al., *British Economic Growth*, pp. 126–8 (table 3.21).
54 G. R. J. Jones, 'Post-Roman Wales', in H. P. R. Finberg (ed.), *AgHist.*, vol. I, part II: *A.D. 43–1042* (Cambridge, 1972), pp. 350–1.
55 Jones, 'Post-Roman Wales', pp. 350–1.
56 Jones, 'Post-Roman Wales', pp. 331–2; on the endemic culture of systematic devastation see D. Stephenson, *Medieval Wales, c.1050–1332: Centuries of Ambiguity* (Cardiff, 2019), pp. 47–54.
57 McCormick, 'The Decline of the Cow', 210.
58 C. Thomas, 'Field Name Evidence in the Reconstruction of Medieval Settlement Nuclei in North Wales', *NLWJ*, 21 (1980), 345. See also C. Thomas, 'A Cultural-ecoogical Model of Agrarian Colonization in Upland Wales', *Landscape History*, 14 (1992), 37–50.
59 R. A. Griffiths, 'William Rees and the modern study of medieval Wales', in R. A. Griffiths and P. R. Schofield (eds), *Wales and the Welsh in the Middle Ages: Essays Presented to J. Beverly Smith* (Cardiff, 2011), pp. 203–20; *SouthWales*.
60 *SouthWales*, pp. xiv–xv, 42–222.

61 See Ll. B. Smith, 'Seignorial Income in the Fourteenth Century: The Arundels in Chirk', *BBCS*, 28 (1979), 443–57.
62 M. Altschul, 'The lordship of Glamorgan and Morgannwg, 1217–1317: I. Glamorgan and Morgannwg under the rule of the De Clare family', in *GlamCH*, pp. 66–7.
63 See P. R. Schofield, 'The family and the village community', in S. H. Rigby (ed.), *A Companion to Britain in the Later Middle Ages* (Oxford, 2003), pp. 26–46.
64 *SouthWales*, p. 31.
65 Jones Pierce, 'Pastoral and agricultural settlements in early Wales', pp. 339–51.
66 Carr, *Medieval Anglesey*, pp. 63–72.; See also Denbigh, where forced exchanges displaced lowland Welsh from 1282. D. H. Owen, 'The Englishry of Denbigh: An English Colony in Medieval Wales', *TransCymm.* (1974/5), 57–76.
67 A. D. M. Barrell and M. H. Brown, 'A Settler Community in Post-conquest Rural Wales', *WHR*, 17 (1995), 339–40.
68 R. R. Davies, 'The social structure of medieval Glamorgan', in *GlamCH*, pp. 285–97.
69 *LordSoc.*, pp. 360–78.
70 M. Davies, 'Field systems of south Wales', in A. R. H. Baker and R. A. Butlin (eds), *Studies of Field Systems in the British Isles* (Cambridge, 1973), p. 483.
71 Davies, 'Field systems of south Wales', p. 483.
72 Thomas, 'Field Name Evidence', 340–56, esp. 345.
73 *AgeCon.*, pp. 146–7.
74 *AgeCon.*, pp. 146–7.
75 *AgeCon.*, p. 149.
76 G. R. J. Jones, 'The Distribution of Medieval Settlement in Anglesey', *TransAng.* (1955), 36, 50–3.
77 Hatcher and Bailey, *Modelling the Middle Ages*, p. 29.
78 S. Rippon, 'Wetland reclamation on the Gwent Levels: dissecting a historic landscape', in N. Edwards (ed.), *Landscape and Settlement in Medieval Wales* (Oxford, 1997), pp. 13, 23–5.
79 Rippon, 'Wetland reclamation', pp. 22–3.
80 M. Lieberman, *The March of Wales, 1067–1300* (Cardiff, 2008), p. 42.
81 *AgeCon.*, p. 147.

82 Kissock, 'Settlement and society', pp. 74–5; *SouthWales*, pp. 142–3.
83 Kissock, 'Settlement and society', p. 75.
84 Kissock, 'Settlement and society', p.75; Howells, 'The countryside', pp. 406–9.
85 B. Campbell and L. Barry, 'The population geography of Great Britain c.1290: a provisional reconstruction', in C. Briggs, P. M. Kitson and S. J. Thompson (eds), *Population, Welfare and Economic Change in Britain, 1290–1834* (Woodbridge, 2014), pp. 59, 65, 68.
86 A. Coghlan, 'Roman Invasion Left No Genetic Legacy', *New Scientist*, 225/3013 (2015), 10.
87 Owen, 'The Englishry of Denbigh', 60.
88 L. Thorpe (trans.), *Gerald of Wales: The Journey through Wales and The Description of Wales* (London, 1978), p. 187; Campbell and Berry, 'The population geography', p. 68.
89 *AgeCon.*, p. 148; see also, S. Duffy, 'The Welsh conquest of Ireland', in E. Purcell, P. MacCotter, J. Nyhan and J. Sheehan (eds), *Clerics, Kings and Vikings: Essays on Medieval Ireland in Honour of Donnchadh Ó Corráin* (Dublin, 2015), pp. 103–14; K. Down, 'Colonial society and economy in the high Middle Ages', in A. Cosgrove (ed.), *A New History of Ireland*, II: *Medieval Ireland, 1169–1534* (Oxford, 1993), pp. 439–91.
90 A. Chapman, *Welsh Soldiers in the Middle Ages, 1282–1422* (Woodbridge, 2015), p. 228.
91 Estimate based on a total population of 300,000, c.50% male, a 'fighting age' of 17–35 years of age, and a typical life expectancy c.35 years of age. See, L. Poos, 'Life Expectancy and "Age of First Appearance" in Medieval Manorial Court Rolls', *Local Population Studies*, 37 (1986), 45–52.
92 B. Holden, *Lords of the Central Marches: English Aristocracy and Frontier Society, 1087–1265* (Oxford, 2008), pp. 54–7.
93 Jones Pierce, 'Medieval Cardiganshire', p. 314.
94 K. Williams-Jones, *The Merioneth Lay Subsidy Roll, 1292–3* (Cardiff, 1976), pp. lxiii–lxiv.
95 Williams-Jones, *The Merioneth Lay Subsidy*, p. lxiii; R. I. Jack, 'Records of Denbighshire lordships, II: The Lordship of Dyffryn Clwyd in 1324', *DHST*, 17 (1968), 31–9; see also, Barrell and Brown, 'A Settler Community', 332–55.
96 Miller and Hatcher, *Medieval England: Rural*, p. 89.

97 B. Campbell, *English Seigniorial Agriculture, 1250–1450* (Cambridge, 2000), pp. 228–31, 250.
98 Armstrong, 'Research briefing: the farming sector', 6.
99 Jack, 'I. Farming techniques', pp. 414, 422, 426.
100 Miller and Hatcher, *Medieval England: Rural*, p. 89; H. L. Gray, *English Field Systems* (Cambridge, Mass., 1915), pp. 70–3.
101 Miller and Hatcher, *Medieval England: Rural*, p. 89; Jack, 'I. Farming techniques', p. 427.
102 B. Campbell, 'Arable Productivity in Medieval England: Some Evidence from Norfolk', *EcHR*, 43 (1983), 396–400.
103 M. F. Stevens, 'The Great Famine in Dyffryn Clwyd, 1315–22', *DHST*, 63 (2015), 24; C. Thomas, 'Thirteenth-century Farm Economies in North Wales', *Agricultural History Review*, 16 (1968), 3.
104 Thomas, 'Thirteenth-century farm economies', 12.
105 Stevens, 'The Great Famine', p. 24; The National Archives (TNA), PRO SC 2/215/71–SC 2/216/5.
106 F. V. Emery, 'West Glamorgan Farming, circa 1580–1620, [part] I', *NLWJ*, 9 (1956), 397; F. V. Emery, 'West Glamorgan Farming, circa 1580–1620, [part] II', *NLWJ*, 10 (1957), 29, 32.
107 Jack, 'I. Farming techniques', pp. 470–5.
108 Campbell, 'Arable Productivity', 382–3.
109 Jack, 'I. Farming techniques', pp. 449–50.
110 Jack, 'I. Farming techniques', p. 453.
111 Jack, 'I. Farming techniques', p. 458.
112 Thomas, 'Thirteenth-century Farm Economies', 12–13.
113 Thomas, 'Thirteenth-century Farm Economies', 8.
114 P. Slavin, 'The Great Bovine Pestilence and its Economic and Environmental Consequences in England and Wales', *EcHR*, 65 (2012), 1260–1.
115 M. M. Postan, 'Village Livestock in the Thirteenth Century', *EcHR*, 15 (1962), 242–3,
116 Postan, 'Village Livestock', 238, 241, 247; Campbell and Overton have indirectly expressed doubts regarding the notion of a livestock 'insufficiency', suggesting, on the basis of Norfolk evidence, that stocking densities have not yet been shown to have related directly to relative changes in total farmland or cereal production, and that from the thirteenth century livestock offered greater scope for

commercial, market-based development than arable agriculture, though this potential was probably not widely realised. B. Campbell and M. Overton, 'A New Perspective on Medieval and Early Modern Ariculture: Six Centuries of Norfolk Farming, c.1250–c.1850', *P&P*, 141 (1993), 76, 83–6 (esp. 85); see also, M. Overton, and B. Campbell, 'Norfolk Livestock Farming 1250–1740: A Comparative Study of Manorial Accounts and Probate Inventories', *Journal of Historical Geography*, 18 (1992), 377–96.

117 Holmes, 'The Future of Animals', 241; Armstrong, 'Research briefing: the farming sector', 6.

118 B. Campbell, 'Benchmarking Medieval Economic Development: England, Wales, Scotland and Ireland, c.1290', *EcHR*, 61 (2008), 931, table 16.

119 L. H. Nelson, *The Normans in South Wales, 1070–1171* (London, 1966), p. 170.

120 J. Bolton, *Money in the Medieval English Economy, 973–1498* (Manchester, 2012), pp. 113–22.

121 M. Allen, *Mints and Money in Medieval England* (Cambridge, 2012), pp. 23–6, 390–1; there exists, in the British Museum, a single coin bearing the name of Welsh prince Hywel Dda (904–49/50), but this is a Wessex-type penny, probably struck in the Chester mint at the will of the English king to honour Hywel as a *subregulus* and ally. D. M. Dykes, 'Seventeenth-century Glamorgan Trade Tokens', *Morgannwg*, 10 (1966), 34.

122 P. Guest, 'The Early Monetary History of Roman Wales: Identity, Conquest and Acculturation on the Imperial Fringe', *Britannia*, 39 (2008), 33–58.

123 T. Jones Pierce, 'The growth of commutation in Gwynedd in the thirteenth century', in *WelshSoc.*, pp. 103–26.

124 Griffiths, 'William Rees', p. 207.

125 E. A. Lewis, *The Medieval Boroughs of Snowdonia* (London, 1912).

126 Lewis, *The Medieval Boroughs*, p. 168.

127 Lewis, *The Medieval Boroughs*, p. 175.

128 M. Beresford, *New Towns of the Middle Ages: Town Plantation in England, Wales and Gascony* (New York, 1967).

129 R. H. Hilton, 'Small Town Life in England before the Black Death', *P&P*, 105 (1984), 56; R. H. Hilton, 'Low-level urbanization: the

Early History, Conquest and Colonisation, 1067–1315   51

seigneurial borough of Thornbury in the Middle Ages', in Z. Razi and R. Smith (eds), *Medieval Society and the Manor Court* (Oxford, 1996), pp. 482–5.
130   *Towns*, pp. 242–7, 101–5.
131   K. D. Lilley, *Urban Life in the Middle Ages, 1000–1450* (Basingstoke, 2002), p. 80.
132   Lilley, *Urban Life*, pp. 48–52.
133   Lilley, *Urban Life*, 80–3; M. F. Stevens, 'Anglo-Welsh towns of the early fourteenth century: a survey of urban origins, property-holding and ethnicity', in *UrbanCult.*, pp. 137–62; see also, M. Bateson, 'The Laws of Breteuil', *The English Historical Review*, 15 and 16 (1900–1), 15/73–8, 302–18, 496–523, 754–7; 16/92–110, 332–45.
134   Stevens, 'Anglo-Welsh towns', p. 141.
135   Bolton, *Money*, p. 141 and ensuing discussion.
136   Stevens, 'Anglo-Welsh towns', p. 141.
137   Bolton, *Money*, pp. 141, 162; B. Campbell, *The Great Transition: Climate, Disease and Society in the Late-Medieval World* (Cambridge, 2016), p. 107.
138   S. Letters et al. (eds), *Gazetteer of Markets and Fairs in England and Wales to 1516*, 2 vols, List and Index Society, special series, 32 and 33 (Kew, 2003).
139   A. J. Taylor, *The Welsh Castles of Edward I* (London, 1986), p. 119.
140   *AgeCon.*, p. 350.
141   *Towns*, p. 16; Stevens, 'Anglo-Welsh towns', p. 141.
142   *Towns*, p. 23; D. Palliser, 'Introduction', in D. Palliser (ed.), *Cambridge Urban History of Britain*, vol. I: *c.600–1540* (Cambridge, 2000), p. 4.
143   See, for example, S. H. Rigby, *Boston, 1086–1225: A Medieval Boom Town* (Lincoln, 2017), p. 65.

Chapter two

THE MEDIEVAL ECONOMY AT ITS APEX, 1282–1348

Industry and commerce

THE DECADES either side of 1300 embodied the economy of Wales at its peak gross productivity with respect to the castle, the Englishry, the Welshry and towns. This is not to say that Wales was a wealthy place, but that it had a greater population and larger number of urban markets, generating higher landlord and borough incomes, than it would until the earliest phases of industrialisation in south Wales, some centuries in the future. Bruce Campbell's Herculean efforts to benchmark the economies of England, Scotland, Ireland and Wales at the close of the thirteenth century suggest that Wales had an overall population density of 37 persons per square mile (PPSM) and a lowland population density of about 92 PPSM. This was second to England, which had an overall population density of 70 PPSM and a lowland population density of 101 PPSM.[1] The per capita wealth of people living in Wales, as measured through the proxy of ecclesiastical wealth – itself derived overwhelmingly from tithes and agricultural production – lagged behind England and Scotland, at just 4.2 pence per person compared with 6.4 pence per person in Scotland and 7.7 pence per person in England.² Only Anglo-Ireland fared worse than Wales, at 3.3 pence per person.

Yet when compared to its neighbours, it is fair to say that the economy of Wales was growing rapidly in the decades following the final conquest of 1282. In a path-breaking article of 1903, Edward Lewis examined 'The Development of Industry and Commerce in Wales' before the 1536 Act of Union.³ Lewis emphasised the importance of native smiths and carpenters as the only pre-conquest craftsmen with specialised skills, and the 'domestic character' of other crafts, for example, the groom who probably made his own halters and the ploughman who fashioned and repaired his own plough.⁴ Thus, he described the extensive building works and urbanisation of post-conquest Wales as heralding a 'passing from the economy of timber to the economy of stone', spurring the exploitation of the mineral resources of Wales, namely, stone, lime, slate, sea coal and lead.⁵ Importantly, the capital investment necessary to exploit these resources was made possible by the stimulus of conquest itself and the flood of silver with which it coincided, as described above.

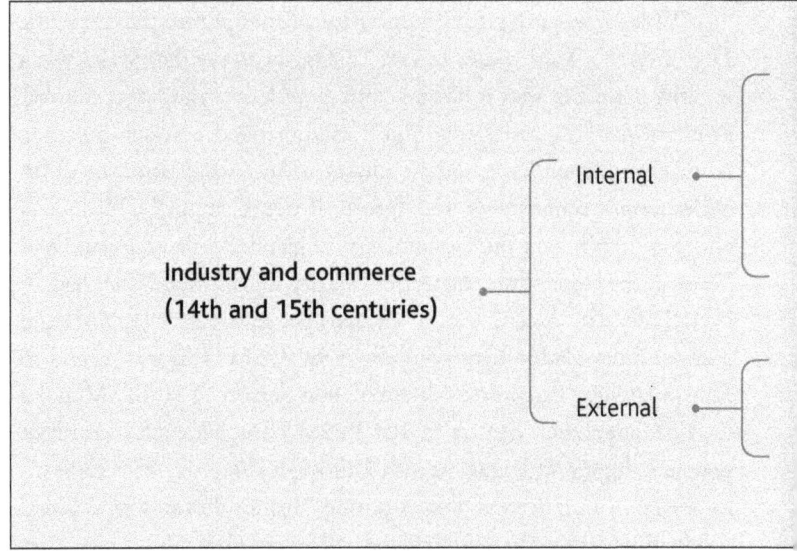

Figure 1. The economy of Wales, as supervised from 'the castle'.

Lewis devised a diagram of the economy of Wales which, with only modest updating, still serves to help us visualise medieval industry and commerce (figure 1). Keeping in mind that, particularly in marcher lordships, all economic activity was directly or indirectly regulated from 'the castle', Lewis separated the internal and external (import/export) economic activities of Wales. Enhancing Lewis's schema, the activities that comprised these two categories of economic activity can then be attributed, in the main, to the residents of the Welshry, of the Englishry or of the towns of Wales.

Internal trade absorbed the vast majority of agricultural output surplus to the subsistence needs of the 80 per cent of people who resided in the countryside, as opposed to a town. However, as today, towns would have contained a hugely disproportionate amount of the country's movable wealth, which was concentrated there by trade. Agriculture in rural areas below 500 to 600 feet (the upper elevation limit for the cultivation of wheat; 58 per cent of Wales lies over 500 feet), especially in Englishries, was orientated towards the production wherever possible of wheat, the most important 'cash crop' of the medieval marketplace.[6]

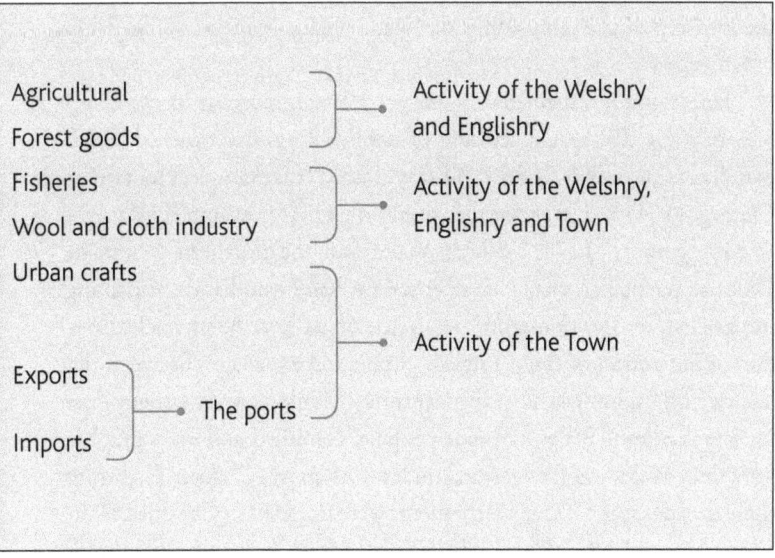

Source: Based on the 'table' in Lewis, 'The development of industry', p. 136.

This was supplemented with the growing of lower-value grains and foodstuffs, especially oats – sometimes in larger quantities than wheat – as well as rye, barley, peas, vetches and beans, and the rearing of cows, sheep and smaller livestock, such as pigs and chickens (see above, Chapter 1, The impact of rural colonisation).[7] Upland areas, often associated with a formal or de facto Welshry, demonstrate just the opposite, focusing on the rearing of bovine livestock, especially cows, for sale in Welsh towns and export to the larger English population centres of Chester, Shrewsbury, Hereford, Gloucester and Bristol.[8] From the early fourteenth century this was supplemented, and in some areas replaced, by the intensive rearing of sheep for the production of wool (see below). The growing of grain was of secondary importance in upland areas and focused on oats, which are better suited to cooler and rainier upland elevations. Lowland and upland communities had a symbiotic economic relationship, insofar as peasant farmers in each area had a diet indicative of their own produce (grains versus dairy and meat), and needed to trade with the other in order to supplement their own produce. It is not by chance that most marcher lordships contained a market town where upland and lowland zones converged, such as Oswestry (Shropshire) in the lordship of the same name, or Neath (Glamorgan) in the lordship of Gower.

Forest goods, especially timber, were also important to the economy of rural Wales. A succession of English kings had ordered Welsh woodlands cleared, at first for military reasons (for example, Henry II at Ceiriog, 1164) and later 'for the common weal' (for example, Edward I at Montgomery, 1278).[9] North Wales and the northern March of Wales, in particular, were characterised by dense woodlands, and along the English border numerous new settlements were being hacked out during the period of rapid English population expansion between the late twelfth and mid-fourteenth centuries. While new-settlement data for late medieval Wales have not yet been compiled and demographic growth in Wales was likely more modest (see above, Chapter 1), during these decades some 77 new settlements were founded in Cheshire, 47 in Shropshire and 18 in Herefordshire, amounting to thousands of acres cleared of saleable timber and underwood.[10] This is then reflected in the building of houses on both sides of the northern Anglo-Welsh border, with the construction of hall houses built mostly or exclusively in timber, at great cost, financed through a combination of credit and wealth accumulated over generations.[11] Meanwhile, in south-west Wales, which was less densely forested, houses were built largely in stone.

The forests of Wales also contained modest mineral deposits that were increasingly exploited. These included, in Glamorgan, the silver, lead and iron mines noted in 1227, in Flintshire the licensing of Flint burgesses to mine lead in 1284 and the emergence of a lead-mining community at Holywell by 1302, and in Cardiganshire the licensing of lead mining near Aberystwyth in 1312 and the suggestive appearance of silver inspectors at Cardigan in 1340.[12] Sea coal and inland surface coal (sometimes also called 'sea coal') were exploited in both north and south Wales, in Flintshire and Pembrokeshire.[13] On Anglesey, mill stones renowned for their quality were quarried, traded across north Wales and exported at least as far as Dublin.[14] But, apart from Anglesey stone, these products were overwhelmingly absorbed by internal trade, and additional resources, such as Spanish iron, were frequently imported either directly from abroad, or from the English border towns of Chester, Shrewsbury, Hereford, Gloucester and Bristol, to supplement local production.[15]

Fisheries may be divided into inland and coastal fisheries. Inland fisheries harnessed as sources of revenue, such as ponds or streams with weirs, were ubiquitous throughout medieval Britain. Major landholders typically possessed fisheries and could require their bond tenants to maintain their weirs, as was required of the bishop of Bangor's tenants.[16] Coastal fisheries could similarly be maintained; the bishop of Bangor, for example, also owned the fisheries around the Skerries Islands, north-west of Anglesey, where fish and seals were taken.[17] Stone sea weirs, called *goredi*, an ancient method of catching fish, existed at numerous points along the Welsh coast in the Middle Ages, as in the Menai Strait, Caernarfon Bay and Cardigan Bay near Aberarth.[18] Coastal fisheries required adequate landing places or safe harbours out of which to operate, and suitable locations, some of ancient usage, ringed the coast of medieval Wales, often becoming regionally important towns because the same safe harbours in which fish could be landed served equally to land men for trade or war. Cardiff and Carmarthen are examples of ports suitable for landing fish, near Roman forts likely to have been supplied in part from the sea, which began to enjoy a second life from at least the late eleventh century when occupied and fortified by Norman incomers.[19] Fishing villages also constituted rare, less-than-fully-agrarian nucleated communities in native Wales, and were natural foci at which to nurture urban development, as the latter-day princes of Gwynedd attempted to do at Pwllheli and Nefyn on the Llŷn Peninsula in the thirteenth century.[20] Herring was the most prized commercial fish to be had on the Welsh coast, with Beaumaris, Barmouth and Aberaeron in north Wales, and Pembroke, Haverford and especially Tenby in south Wales, the main herring ports.[21] Nevertheless, despite the notable twenty-three fishing boats of Aberystwyth recorded as working Cardigan Bay in 1348, seemingly in pursuit of herring, Wales probably did little more than meet its own needs most of the year.[22] While Anglo-Norman conquerors were keen to tax herring boats, the Welsh fisheries were slow to commercialise and never developed as fully as those in south-western England, something Maryanne Kowaleski has attributed 'in part' to 'the limited investment possible in the uncertain political climate in Wales'.[23]

However, major investment in infrastructure was made across Wales in the period between Edward I's 1282 war of conquest, and the depopulation caused by the Black Death in 1348–9. Lords invested in bridges to aid in the smooth transit of goods. For example, stone bridges linking England and Wales were built over the Monnow at Monmouth in 1272 – topped with a gate (suitable for collecting tolls) between 1297 and 1315 – and over the Dee at Holt in 1339. At the same time, the cloth industry in Wales and the March was aided, between 1301 and 1349, by the construction of at least forty-nine new fulling mills for the softening and finishing of raw cloth. While it is often difficult to determine when a mill was first constructed, more than seventy-eight grain-grinding and fulling watermills have been located within the lordship of Gower alone, a majority of which may have pre-modern roots.[26]

A key area of the Welsh economy that grew prodigiously from the early fourteenth century was trade in wool and inexpensive cloth. The rearing of increasingly large flocks of sheep, alongside or in place of cattle, was well underway in Wales by 1300. For example, in the medieval lordship of Dyffryn Clwyd (Denbighshire), the lord's demesne flock numbered 2,000–3,000 and the aggregated tenant flocks nearly as many, with several private flocks numbering between 100 and 240.[27] Similar seigniorial flocks appeared in the lordships of Clun (Shropshire) and Brecon, on the lands of Tintern Abbey (Chepstow lordship) and elsewhere.[28] While the medieval cloth industry did not always develop where wool was produced, there were obvious benefits to the local economy where it did so. In Dyffryn Clwyd, weaving as supplementary economic activity on rural farmsteads – often piecework put out by professional urban weavers – was sufficiently common by 1330 to inspire local officials to introduce an assize (effectively a tax) on weaving outside the lordship's borough of Ruthin, which was paid in that year by 138 people, 136 of whom were women.[29] Within Ruthin, at about the same time, a handful of female combers, knitters, burlers and kell (hairnet) makers assisted and complimented the work of around six professional male weavers, a dyer, a couple of fullers, a shearman, a blanket maker, two mercers, a draper and a dozen tailors.[30] These cloth workers and traders, plus other necessary part-time workers such as spinners of thread, comprised over 10 per cent of Ruthin's population of about 500, a situation that would have been mirrored elsewhere. The chief markets for Welsh cloth were in the English border towns of Shrewsbury, Hereford, Ludlow and, in particular, Bristol.[31]

Urban craft and industry depended on the close integration with rural producers found in the cloth industry. For instance, the large amount of livestock reared in the countryside, especially in the upland Welshries, gave rise to a complementary trade in leather goods. Again using Ruthin as an example, in the early fourteenth century the borough housed about ten skinners and tanners, three glovers and well over a dozen cobblers, making the borough an important regional producer of shoes.[32] If one considers that most of these craftsmen would have employed one or more labourers, leather industries too occupied more than 10 per cent of Ruthin's urban population. Vocational name data from Welsh towns illustrates a typical range of medieval small-town industries, particularly those stemming from metal working and wood working, and includes non-specialised occupational bynames, such a smith and carpenter, as well as specialised bynames such as armourer and wheelwright (or their Welsh and Latin equivalents). Between the mid-thirteenth and mid-fourteenth centuries, towns across Wales that successfully capitalised on emergent industries and trade grew rapidly, with the most prosperous seeing substantial town-property subdivision and accumulation by wealthy families.[33]

Ports grew in this period, but the work of those in marcher lordships is poorly represented in surviving documentation, and royal boroughs little better served.[34] Customs accounts, pertaining mainly to royal boroughs, are a crucial source of information and were first surveyed by Lewis over a century ago.[35] During the reigns of Edward I and II (1272–1327), Cardigan, a royal borough, and Haverfordwest, a lordship borough, were the chief ports from which wool was exported with royal oversight, including customs collection and formal debt registration from 1284, as staple ports with licence to deal in wool, pelts, leather, lead and tin.[36] In 1326 the royal foundation of New Carmarthen which, together with the adjoining native monastic town of Old Carmarthen and nearby episcopal town of Abergwili, had a combined population of about 1,500–2,000 souls, was recognised as a royal staple port.[37] Cardiff, being of a similar size to the cluster of towns at Carmarthen, also won recognition as a staple in 1326.[38] A list of staples compiled in the same year does not include Cardigan, whose merchants thereafter registered their customs through Carmarthen staple.[39] And, not long thereafter, Haverfordwest and Cardiff lost their staple status in 1332 when the Crown decided that only royal towns ought to have the privilege, though Haverford exports continued to be enrolled at Carmarthen until at least 1360.[40] No customs were levied in the Crown's north Wales Principality until 1339, when Caernarfon, at the heart of an urban cluster of Menai Straits towns including Bangor and Beaumaris, became a staple in association with Rhuddlan.[41] This configuration of licensed overseas trade through royal boroughs, with Caernarfon serving north Wales and Carmarthen serving south Wales, would then hold until after the Black Death. While designation of a town as a staple did not necessarily equate to prosperity, its effect in channelling certain kinds of trade, such as wool, through a particular port with a facility to register credit arrangements before royal officials, must have encouraged local economic growth. However, royal officials were all but powerless to force marcher lords and their tenants to direct their trade through staple ports. Chepstow, for example, prospered specifically because goods could be unloaded there, in a marcher lordship, at a lower custom on merchandise – one twelfth or less that of royal custom in Bristol – and then transported overland to England.[42] The numerous small ports of Wales supplied all corners of the country's new network of towns with a rich variety of imported goods, which were otherwise all but unavailable in a far corner of Europe. And while the attitudes of early fourteenth-century Welsh poets, such as Dafydd ap Gwilym, towards towns were 'ambiguous', Dafydd praised 'the radiant town' of Newborough (Anglesey), and poets balanced their criticisms of the unique opportunities for vice that towns offered with a fascination for these new emporia which offered 'every ware from foreign lands'.[43]

Urbanisation and immigration

While the rural colonisation of Wales by English immigrants probably had a modest effect on population growth, as discussed in Chapter 1 above, the introduction of towns in Wales can be said to have definitively increased local population densities. Whereas Wales had no discernible urban centres at the time of fitz Osbern's invasion of 1067 and subsequent foundation of Monmouth and Chepstow, by 1300 Wales contained just over 100 small towns, in which 20 per cent of the population resided (see above, Chapter 1, Commutation and urbanisation).[44] Tenant and taxpayer lists indicate that c.1300 these towns housed about 46,500 persons, of whom about 8,000 were Welsh, that is 17 per cent.[45]

While nearly all people in Wales would have had access to a market by *c.*1300, this 17 per cent share of urban population growth was fuelled by native Welsh entry into the new burgess class of traders, mostly in modest, undefended, interior market villages. Where chartered borough status was granted to a pre-existing Welsh community, or where an equivalent package of trading privileges was granted to a rural crossroads, a village by a prominent church or other meeting point that grew organically into a small trading community, native Welsh might well account for more than half of residents.[46] For example in 1293, with respect to formally reconfigured pre-existing Welsh settlements, native Welsh comprised 62 per cent of a population of about of about 50 (8 of 13 tax payers) at Llanidloes (Montgomeryshire) and 77 per cent of a population of about 90 (17 of 22 tax payers) at Cilgerran (Pembrokeshire).[47] Even more strongly Welsh dominated were the communities of Lampeter (Cardiganshire), where Welsh persons comprised 90 per cent of a population of about 90 (19 of 21 property holders in 1303), and Llangadog (Carmarthenshire), where Welsh persons comprised 97 per cent of a population of about 100 (32 of 33 property holders in 1326).[48] However, these smaller settlements with a strong Welsh influence account for only about a quarter of towns in Wales, an even smaller share of the urban population, and, by extension, a similarly small share of economic output.

In contrast, the backbone of the new urban network of Wales was made up of larger towns, typically those founded on greenfield sites or anew in parallel to pre-existing Welsh villages, and defended by castles, where the vast majority of residents were English.[49] English townspeople amounted, by 1300, to about 38,500 first-, second- or third-generation incomers to Wales, that is, 83 per cent to town dwellers and 13 to 15 per cent of the 250,000–300,000 persons living in Wales.[50] They dominated the eight settlements with probable populations in excess of 1,000.

The largest of these settlements were Cardiff (Glamorgan), and the cluster of urban communities at Carmarthen (Carmarthenshire). Cardiff was the seat of the lordship of Glamorgan, the most productive single lordship in medieval Wales, which was valued at

£1,276 per annum in 1317.⁵¹ The town alone was valued at £127 9s. 11d in a royal inquiry of 1295, similar to the total value of the small lordship of Wigmore on the Herefordshire border.⁵² In 1281 officials rendered account for the rents of 380 burgages, rising to over 400 by 1295, suggesting a population approaching 2,000.⁵³ But that population, already spreading beyond the south and east gates of the city walls, appears to have been overwhelmingly English; the town jurors who assembled the 1295 inquiry were exclusively English, as were city officials and known property owners of the time.⁵⁴ This suggests that Cardiff was a key, or even the main, entry point to south Wales for English immigrants, and a recipient of the material and human capital they brought with them. It was also a privately held staple port from 1326 until 1332, when, as noted above, the Crown decided that only royal boroughs ought to enjoy that privilege.⁵⁵ This combination of wealth and ethnic exclusivity was no doubt a factor in Owain Glyndŵr's decision not just to sack the borough in 1404, but, according to the *Eulogium Eistoriarum*, to burn it entirely apart from Crokerton Street and the Franciscan friary there.⁵⁶

The urban cluster at Carmarthen was a conglomeration of the monastic settlement of Old Carmarthen, the adjoining Norman castellated borough of New Carmarthen and the nearby episcopal settlement of Abergwili, all trading within sight of each other along the north bank of the River Towy. Together they contained 335 burgages, many of which were subdivided for multiple occupancy, and a population probably in excess of 1,500, of which over two-thirds were English, as suggested by personal-name evidence.⁵⁷ New Carmarthen was the administrative centre of the post-conquest royal Principality in south Wales and one of only two staple ports in Wales from 1332 to 1353 (together with Caernarfon), when, following the depopulation of the Black Death, the 1353 Statute of the Staple designated it the *only* staple port in Wales; the statute also gave Welsh and Irish merchants permission to use English staple ports, Bristol being the only west coast example.⁵⁸

The six other towns with a population probably in excess of 1,000 were similarly English dominated: Holt (Denbighshire), Cowbridge (Glamorgan), Haverfordwest (Pembrokeshire), Chepstow (Monmouthshire), Usk (Monmouthshire), Newport (Monmouthshire) and Monmouth, (Monmouthshire).[59] Together the eight largest towns of Wales had a population approximating the combined population of the fifty smallest towns. They accounted for about 20 per cent of the total urban population, and nearly 5 per cent of the total population, of Wales.

The location of the larger towns of Wales, along the highly Anglicised south coast, and on the extreme north-east and south-east border with England, is not coincidental. These towns were populated overwhelmingly by English immigrants moving west in search of a better life. The same is true of the forty or so middling towns of Wales, with populations of about 500–600, such as Denbigh (Denbighshire) or Tenby (Pembrokeshire). Those promising settlements most accessible to English immigrants by land or sea, on the fertile coastal plains and in the river valleys of Wales, received the heaviest immigration, with immigrant numbers diminishing the further one journeyed into the less accessible, poorer interior. Plainly speaking, this was a human migration from an area of higher population density to one of lower population density, and the economic benefits of urbanisation and associated commercialisation spread across Wales in conjunction with that population redistribution.

This is significant for a number of reasons. Institutional urbanism, from the slender grant of a periodic market to the robust creation by charter of a privileged guild merchant, could and did serve to spread concepts of urbanity, to induce commutation and to facilitate a 'money economy' in Wales. But the growth of any more than the skeletal outline of urban life required those new urban forms to be populated. Even in times of general population growth, towns required extensive immigration simply to maintain numbers in opposition to the heightened mortality – especially infant mortality – associated with the close-quarters living of town life.[60] In Wales, however, a resource-constrained and largely stagnant native Welsh population failed to fill up and to grow new towns, even those that were overwhelmingly or exclusively populated by Welsh inhabitants.

Only those towns favourably positioned to serve as outlets for an increasing English population grew substantially. This was undeniably in part because they tended to be those towns most favourably positioned for commerce, such as Cardiff and Carmarthen, with broad arable hinterlands and access to seaborne trade. But equally, this is because they were expressions of an English demographic crisis. The precocious expansion of the urban network in England from 1066 to 1300 has frequently, and at times somewhat uncritically, been attributed to the 'growth of trade everywhere in England, and at all levels'.[61] But as Britnell argued, the more than doubling of the English population between 1180 and 1330 pushed an increasing number of families who could not be fed from their scant agricultural lands into 'self-employment and dependence upon trade, and this is what the growth and multiplication of English towns and markets between 1180 and 1330 demonstrates'.[62] English urbanisation was then both a product and a cause of economic growth; Beresford estimated that 153 new towns were created in England between 1066 and 1300 at an average rate of about 6 per decade, peaking at 12 per decade 1191–1230, as a land-hungry English population streamed into new settlements that, in turn, generated trade.[63] The flurry of thirteenth-century urban expansion and new-town foundation in Wales was not an indicator of endemic Welsh demographic growth but rather reflected primarily the exotic influence of English immigration. The population of Wales increased modestly as a result of immigration-fuelled urbanisation, the net increase reflected by the 20 per cent of persons living in towns *c.*1300. But this demographic growth, and the economic benefits thereof, was externally driven and in no way suggests a groundswell of domestic fertility or productivity.

Lordship and society

Increases in thirteenth- and early fourteenth-century seigniorial revenues in Wales, as indicated in accounts that become available from shortly *after* Anglo-Norman conquest, are best attributed to recovery from conflict and the elaboration of seigniorial administration rather than genuine increases in peasant productivity – defined here as increases in agricultural output leading to demographic and economic growth. The absence of detailed accounts from any part of pre-conquest Wales serves to frustrate the modern scholar of the native economy. But the end of regular and substantial intra-Welsh and Anglo-Welsh conflict in Wales following the conquest of 1282–3 unburdened the economy of the losses inevitably associated with frequent raids and incursions. For example, the Welsh kingdoms of Gwynedd and Powys engaged in no less than twenty-five armed conflicts between 1132 and 1282, while a similar number of Anglo-Welsh conflicts occurred over the same period.[64] As discussed in Chapter 1, native Wales underwent 'a veritable agrarian revolution in the years between 1000 and 1300', with the growth of the semi-free or free *gwely*, as both a territorial and a social unit, playing a role in better exploiting marginally croppable and upland areas.[65] But this was primarily a revolution of organisation that, among other things, would have led to larger numbers of free *gwelyau* with an obligation to render military service, rather than acting as a catalyst for greater agricultural productivity.

The equally revolutionary transformation of discrete parcels of Welsh territory into marcher lordships, usually with designated or de facto Welshries, produced a novel body of economic records that grew in volume and detail over the twelfth and thirteenth centuries. From these it is possible to estimate that income from the lordship of Glamorgan grew, as a proportion of the total income of the Clare Earls of Gloucester and Hereford, from 15 per cent in the late twelfth century, to 23 per cent in 1266 and finally to 40 per cent in 1317.[66] Glamorgan is somewhat exceptional, as the lordship also grew in size over this period, but it is fair to say that most seigniorial incomes in Wales grew substantially up to *c*.1348. Rents provided the main source of stable and regular revenue from marcher lordships. But, unlike England, where steadily rising seigniorial profits were fuelled by rising rents associated with increasing population density, the two main drivers of sharply increasing seigniorial income in Wales were judicial lordship and arbitrary taxation in the form of gifts, grants and subsidies.[67]

'Judicial lordship' describes the income that marcher lords derived from lordship courts, such as fees to use the courts, a share of debts recovered there, fines for breaking village ordinances (e.g. untended animals), payments to re-enter the lord's peace after crimes, the sale of convicted felons' goods and moneys collected by lordship officials, often at farm (see Chapter 1, The agrarian economy before the Black Death), such as tolls, marriage fees and death duties. In England, judicial functions and the revenues they generated were divided between a number of jurisdictions and recipients, local and royal. Village affairs were regulated in the manor court, with greater civil matters going before the hundred court, county court or Court of Common Pleas at Westminster, and felony crimes, such as rape or murder, being prosecuted by royal Eyre, royal commissions of Goal Delivery, or at the Court of King's Bench at Westminster. In marcher lordships, all of these jurisdictions were consolidated in the hands of the lord, who received all the revenues arising from them.

Arbitrary taxation in marcher lordships 'masqueraded under a series of largely euphemistic names – "gifts", "aids", "tallages", "mises", "subsidies"'.[68] In England royal taxation, following the Magna Carta of 1215, required the consent of the 'common counsel', which was eventually granted by parliament, and usually took the form of subsidies calculated as a proportion of the value of a householder's movable goods. Here, the casual revenues of lordship were limited to a number of ancient and reasonably predictable dues such as feudal aids and scutages as when the lord's son was knighted or the lord undertook military service; this latter due was usually commuted to a payment in lieu of service well before 1300 and the cost passed on to tenants. When these English taxes were imported to Wales they became arbitrary in the hands of 'lords royal' in Wales, and supplemented revenues arising from both rents and the intensive collection of recast and 'farmed' traditional Welsh dues such as *amobr*.

In Davies's words, 'financially, marcher lordship *was* [Davies's emphasis] different: the profits of justice and casual revenue assured that it was so ... we are here at the very heart of the distinctiveness of marcher lordship.'[69] By the 1330s, rents accounted for just 19 per cent of the revenues of the Mortimer lordships of the middle March whilst in 1386–8 they made up just 41 per cent of the income of the lordship of Kidwelly.[70] Most of the lords' remaining income came from judicial lordship and the casual revenue of arbitrary taxation. For example, these generated 46 per cent of gross income in Brecon lordship (1337–46) and 43 per cent in Chirk (1340–50).[71] Moreover, the burden of supporting these income streams fell disproportionally on the tenants in Welshries, which were situated in marginally croppable districts. In mostly marginal and upland Brecon, which saw only modest English immigration, judicial lordship and arbitrary taxation amounting to almost £4,000 was extracted over the years 1337–58.[72] In 1302 about 2,000 Welshmen from Brecon formally swore allegiance to the king, suggesting a total population of about 8,000 persons (with an average household of four). The remainder of this population after the plague of 1348–9, perhaps half to two-thirds, would then pay the lord, in the five years 1352–7, some £400 for assarting lands in Brecon's forests, £66 13s. 4d. for 'wrongful judgements', £500 for evading tolls and £750 for attacking the men of Builth lordship, a total of £1,716 13s. 4d.[73] Over roughly the same period, 1340–58, the major set render of the Welshmen of Brecon to their lord, the by then commuted biennial *commorth*, or cow tribute, doubled in value from a comparatively modest £36 to £81, as both the notional number of cows and the value of each cow was increased.[74] In contrast to Brecon, 73 per cent of the gross revenue of the relatively Anglicised and arable lordship of Monmouth came strictly from rents and farms.[75]

David Walker argued that while the potentially exploitative tone and frequency of taxation in Brecon may smack of heavy-handed lordship, the ability of the Welsh to pay it and the growth of a substantial cross-border trade in cattle and sheep – no doubt needed to generate the coin to meet tax demands – suggest it may not have been overly burdensome.[76] Ultimately, it is impossible to know how onerous households found these financial demands, and taxation may have indirectly stimulated the cattle trade as upland farmers sought to sell beasts to pay taxes.

Collecting even high levels of taxation from lordships need not necessarily have been detrimental to lordship economies if reinvested locally, for example in construction and consumption. But lordship revenues did not often stay in Wales, leaving lordship tenants increasingly generating wealth that was exported to England as post-conquest peace extended into the middle of the fourteenth century. A commercializing

Welsh economy had emerged rapidly in the thirteenth century during the 'flood of silver' into the country that paid for castle construction, soldiers' wages and even an initial burst of infrastructure investment (see Chapter 1, Commutation and urbanisation). As the fourteenth century began to wear on, this flow of silver slowed to a halt, reversed, and began to flow ever more quickly back into England, a status quo that would characterise the following century. Marcher lords' local expenditure on demesne agriculture, castle maintenance, the fees of officials, the costs of holding courts and other lordship works was generally just 10–30 per cent of gross revenue, only a small fraction of which was capital reinvestment, such as the building of a mill or weir, leaving them free to dispose of around three-quarters of income to meet commitments east of the border.[77] As Davies observed, 'There was little thought of capital formation, of investing the profits of lordships in local estates, with the exception of some purchase of stock or the occasional loan to a local merchant. The income was the personal fortune of the lord...'[78] Low levels of landlord reinvestment of profits in their manors, of only around 5 per cent, were also common in England.[79] Particular to Wales was the long-term export of profits, both those used for reinvestment and the conspicuous consumption that characterised the life of the nobility, to England, where resided both the royal household and most marcher lords, or even abroad.[80]

Llinos Smith's analysis of the fourteenth-century accounts of the Arundel lords of Chirk and Bromfield and Yale found that 'harsh' seigniorial financial policy geared towards maximum income extraction marked their relationship with their newer acquisitions in Wales, while they were 'far more prepared to invest heavily in their established eastern possessions', such as their Shropshire manors.[81] Richard II fitz Alan, Earl of Arundel and Surrey (c.1307–1376) was one of the richest men in England at his death, leaving an estate of £72,173, of which £60,180 was ready cash, generated in part by an income of as much as £500 a year (1322–80) from the lordship of Chirk alone.[82] His main expenditures focused on a new range, great hall and chantry at Arundel Castle (Sussex), extensive building work at Shrawardine Castle (Shropshire), a new chapel at Oriel College Oxford, prosecuting Edward III's wars, lending money to the Crown and other magnates for war and other purposes, and commissioning luxury goods such as fine tapestries and silverware in London, Chichester (Sussex), Arras and Paris.[83] Expenditure in Chirk lordship comprised principally the construction of about half a dozen mills and the establishment of a short-lived vaccary at small expense in relation to net lordship revenues.[84]

Thus, even were the profits of judicial lordship and arbitrary taxation not overly irksome and burdensome – Smith describes those at Chirk as increasingly 'capricious . . . untampered by discretion and mercy' – they would inevitably have operated as a form of regressive taxation.[85] Profits increasingly were not reinvested, and substantial agricultural yields, such as the cows yielded by Brecon lordship and driven to English markets, were not consumed locally. This may have exercised some modest restraint on population growth in Wales, felt more strongly the further exporting communities were from their products' ultimate destination, as few farmers of Wales were as able as Brecon's upland pastoralists to access cheaply and directly the English market.

Notes

1 B. Campbell, 'Benchmarking Medieval Economic Development: England, Wales, Scotland and Ireland, c.1290', *EcHR*, 61 (2008), 931, table 16.
2 Campbell, 'Benchmarking Medieval Economic Development', 931, table 16.
3 E. A. Lewis, 'The Development of Industry and Commerce in Wales during the Middle Ages', *TransRoyal*, new series, 17 (1903), 121–73.
4 Lewis, 'The Development of Industry', 126.
5 Lewis, 'The Development of Industry', 128.
6 R. I. Jack, 'I. Farming techniques: H Wales and the Marches', in H. E. Hallman (ed.), *AgHist.*, vol. II: *1042–1350* (Cambridge, 1988), pp. 443.

7   Jack, 'I. Farming techniques', pp. 449–74.
8   Jack, 'I. Farming techniques', pp. 476–96.
9   Lewis, 'The Development of Industry', 139.
10 R. I. Jack, 'New settlement: H Wales and the Marches', in E. H. Hallman (ed.), *AgHist.*, vol. II: *1042–1350* (Cambridge, 1988), pp. 260–71.
11 R. Suggett, 'The interpretation of late medieval houses in Wales', in R. R. Davies and G. H. Jenkins (eds), *From Medieval to Modern Wales: Historical Essays in Honour of Kenneth O. Morgan and Ralph A. Griffiths* (Cardiff, 2004), pp. 84–6.
12 Lewis, 'The Development of Industry', 142, 145, 148; *Towns*, pp. 147–8.
13 *Towns*, p. 146.
14 A. D. Carr, *Medieval Anglesey*, 2nd edn (Llangefni, 2011), pp. 74–6.
15 Lewis, 'The Development of Industry', 148.
16 Carr, *Medieval Anglesey*, p. 77.
17 Carr, *Medieval Anglesey*, p. 77.
18 M. Kowaleski, 'The Commercialization of the Sea Fisheries in Medieval England and Wales', *International Journal of Maritime History*, 15 (2003), 219.
19 Carmarthen had already long been an ecclesiastical possession, and so may have seen some sea traffic; see R. A. Griffiths, 'Carmarthen', in *Boroughs*, pp. 130–63.
20 T. Jones Pierce, 'A Caernarvonshire manorial borough', in *WelshSoc.*, pp. 127–93.
21 Lewis, 'The Development of Industry', 150.
22 Lewis, 'The Development of Industry', 150.
23 Kowaleski, 'The Commercialization of the Sea Fisheries', 220.
24 Royal Commission on the Ancient and Historical Monuments of Wales, NPRN 24219; S. W. Ward, 'A Survey of Holt-Farndon Medieval Bridge', *Cheshire Past: An Annual Review of Archaeology in Cheshire*, 1 (1992), 14.
25 R. I. Jack, 'The Cloth Industry in Medieval Wales', *WHR*, 10 (1980–1), 449.
26 B. Taylor, *Watermills of the Lordship of Gower* (Bishopston, 2009).
27 Jack, 'The Cloth Industry', 457–8.
28 Jack, 'The Cloth Industry', 458.

29 M. F. Stevens, *Urban Assimilation in Post-Conquest Wales: Ethnicity, Gender and Economy in Ruthin, 1282–1348* (Cardiff, 2010), pp. 184–90.
30 Stevens, *Urban Assimilation*, pp. 179 (table 5.1), 232 (table 6.4).
31 Lewis, 'The Development of Industry', 159.
32 Stevens, *Urban Assimilation*, p. 232 (table 6.4).
33 Stevens, *Urban Assimilation*, pp. 44–53.
34 For efforts to work around the general absence of medieval marcher port records, using property deeds and a post-medieval custom book, see, S. Dimmock, 'Haverfordwest: An Exemplar for the Study of Southern Welsh Towns in the Later Middle Ages', *WHR*, 22 (2004), 1–28; S. Dimmock, 'The Custom Book of Chepstow', *Studia Celtica*, 38 (2004), 131–49.
35 E. A. Lewis, 'A Contribution to the Commercial History of Medieval Wales', *Y Cymmrodor*, 24 (1913), 86–188.
36 Lewis, 'The Development of Industry', 151.
37 M. F. Stevens, 'Anglo-Welsh towns of the early fourteenth century: a survey of urban origins, property-holding and ethnicity', in *UrbanCult.*, pp. 152–3; *Towns*, p. 103.
38 D. G. Walker, 'Cardiff', in *Boroughs*, p. 126.
39 Lewis, 'The Development of Industry', 151, n. 2; Lewis, 'A Contribution', 134–40.
40 The collection of royal customs from ports in marcher lordships, when not operating as staples, was dependent on voluntary local cooperation and highly inconsistent. Lewis, 'The Development of Industry', 151; Lewis, 'A Contribution', 102, 138–40.
41 Lewis, 'The Development of Industry', 151.
42 S. Dimmock, 'Urban and Commercial Networks in the Later Middle Ages: Chepstow, Severnside and the Ports of Southern Wales', *Archaeologia Cambrensis*, 152 (2003), 53.
43 D. Johnston, 'Towns in medieval Welsh poetry', in *UrbanCult.*, pp. 95, 98, 100
44 *Towns*, pp. 16, 19–24.
45 *Towns*, p. 24.
46 Stevens, 'Anglo-Welsh towns', p. 141.
47 Stevens, 'Anglo-Welsh towns', pp. 141, 155, 157; *Towns*, pp. 109–10, 170–2.

48 Stevens, 'Anglo-Welsh towns', pp. 141, 156–7; *Towns*, pp. 157–8, 169–70.
49 Stevens, 'Anglo-Welsh towns', p. 141.
50 *Towns*, pp. 23–4.
51 *LordSoc.*, p. 196.
52 *LordSoc.*, p. 196; R. A. Griffiths, 'The medieval boroughs of Glamorgan and medieval Swansea, I: The boroughs of the lordship of Glamorgan', in *GlamCH*, p. 342.
53 Walker, 'Cardiff', pp. 118–19; Griffiths, 'The medieval boroughs', pp. 342–3.
54 Griffiths, 'The medieval boroughs', pp. 342–3.
55 Lewis, 'The Development of Industry', 151.
56 T. B. Pugh, 'The marcher lords of Glamorgan and Morgannwg, 1317–1485', in *GlamCH*, p. 184; F. S. Haydon (ed.), *Eulogium Historiarum sive Temporis: Chronicon ab Orbe Condito Usque ad Annum Domini M.CCC.LXVI, a Monacho Quodam Malmesburiensi Exaratum* (London, 1863), p. 401.
57 Stevens, 'Anglo-Welsh towns', pp. 141, 151–4.
58 Lewis, 'The Development of Industry', 152; *Statutes*, p. 30.
59 *Towns*, p. 23.
60 C. Platt, *The English Medieval Town* (London, 1976), pp. 98–100.
61 Platt, *The English Medieval Town*, p. 26.
62 R. H. Britnell, *The Commercialisation of English Society, 1000–1500*, 2nd edn (Cambridge, 1996), p. 104.
63 M. Beresford, *New Towns of the Middle Ages: Town Plantation in England, Wales and Gascony* (New York, 1967), p. 330.
64 D. Stephenson, *Medieval Powys: Kingdom, Principality and Lordships, 1132–1293* (Woodbridge, 2016), p. 274; D. Stephenson, *Medieval Wales, c.1050–1332: Centuries of Ambiguity* (Cardiff, 2019), pp. 47–54, 104–120
65 T. Jones Pierce, 'Pastoral and agricultural settlements in early Wales', in *WelshSoc.*, p. 339.
66 D. Walker, *Medieval Wales* (Cambridge, 1990), p. 60.
67 Walker, *Medieval Wales*, p. 60.
68 *LordSoc.*, p. 184.
69 *LordSoc.*, p. 187.
70 *LordSoc.*, p. 178.

71 *LordSoc.*, p. 187.
72 *LordSoc.*, p. 185.
73 Walker, *Medieval Wales*, p. 61.
74 *LordSoc.*, p. 192.
75 *LordSoc.*, p. 178.
76 Walker, *Medieval Wales*, p. 61.
77 *LordSoc.*, p. 190.
78 *LordSoc.*, p. 190.
79 S. H. Rigby, *English Society in the Later Middle Ages: Class, Status and Gender* (Houndmills, 1995), p. 128; R. H. Hilton, *The English Peasantry in the Later Middle Ages: The Ford Lectures for 1973 and Related Studies* (Oxford, 1975), pp. 174–214 (chapter x, 'Rent and capital formation in feudal society').
80 On noble expenditure see K. B. McFarlane, *The Nobility of Later Medieval England: The Ford Lectures for 1953 and Related Studies* (Oxford, 1973), pp. 83–101.
81 Ll. B. Smith, 'Seignorial Income in the Fourteenth Century: The Arundels in Chirk', *BBCS*, 28 (1979), 456.
82 Smith, 'Seignorial Income', 449; M. Burtscher, *The Fitzalans: Earls of Arundel and Surrey, Lords of the Welsh Marches, 1267–1415* (Little Logaston, 2008), p. 59.
83 Burtscher, *The Fitzalans*, p. 61–2, 65.
84 Smith, 'Seignorial Income', 456.
85 Smith, 'Seignorial Income, 456.

Chapter three
CRISES AND RESTRUCTURING, 1315–1536

THE STORY OF the Welsh economy between the arrival of the Great Famine of 1315–22 and the Act of Union of England and Wales in 1536 is rarely a happy one. The population collapsed, following famine in 1315–22 and plague in 1348–9 and 1361–2. The old social and economic building block of the Welsh *gwely* crumbled. Law and order declined. Some towns failed completely. Following the Glyndŵr rebellion of 1400–16, the causes of which certainly included economic grievances, Wales became a land that looked to England for economic lifelines, exporting its own people across the border in significant numbers.

The collapse of the *gwely*

The *gwely* came under immediate threat in periods of conquest when escheat and forced exchange broke up lowland extended-family holdings and pushed *gwelyau* into upland Welshries, as happened in the lordship of Denbigh from 1282, while natural disasters would further accelerate their demise.[1] Nevertheless, it was the long-term effect of commercialisation and increased individualism, coming to full fruition only towards the middle decades of the fourteenth century, which ultimately would dissolve the *gwely*. The increasing incompatibility of the *gwely* as a legal-economic unit, based on communal property holding and shared legal and financial responsibility, with the commercialising economy and its emphasis on individual responsibility led Welsh tenants variously to abandon hereditary *gwely* holdings and/or to seek land by English tenure.[2]

The post-conquest legal settlement set out in the 1284 Statute of Wales played an important role in the decline of the *gwely*.[3] Defined by Llinos Smith as 'nothing more (or less) than an outline scheme for the government of the king's lands in Wales', it records that the king 'caused to be rehearsed' before himself and his nobles the 'laws and customs of Wales' and then 'abolished certain of them, [while] some thereof . . . [were] . . . allowed'.[4] While the statute, in theory, took immediate effect within the royal Principality, its adoption by the marcher lords, who collectively controlled the greater part of Wales, would only come about fitfully over the course of the fourteenth and fifteenth centuries.

The native law of Hywel Dda had emphasised communal legal and financial responsibility. For example, in what might broadly be termed 'criminal' law, it preferred compensation to corporal punishment. In instances of proven insult, injury, rape or even unlawful killing, resolution was reached through a compensation payment made by the perpetrator and his (or her) immediate and extended family to the immediate and extended family of the victim, that is to say, a compensation payment from one *gwely* to another. Best researched is the compensation payment for unlawful killing, or *galanas*, to which the perpetrator and his immediate family contributed one-third, the other two-thirds being contributed by paternal and maternal kin sharing the perpetrator's great-grandparents, that is, collaterally as far as fifth cousins or nine degrees of relationship.[5] The victim's immediate and extended family received the payment, distributed in a manner mirroring its collection. The value of the *galanas* was scaled to the victim's social standing (e.g. free/unfree, married/single, etc.), but was generally very substantial or even life-changing. Payments in fourteenth-century north Wales lordships, in compensation for the killing of freemen, tended to be about £24, at a time and in a place where an ox, often a peasant farmer's most valuable possession, was worth about 10s., or one forty-eighth of *galanas*.[6] These payments tied the *gwelyau* together, legally and financially, through the periodic collection and redistribution of substantial sums, with enforcement sought through lordship courts suggesting that it was not unusual for twenty or more kinsmen to be obliged to contribute to a *galanas*.[7] The 1284 Statute of Wales replaced *galanas* with English legal process and individual punishment in royal lands, normally hanging for Crown felony pleas such as homicide. But marcher lords, all of whom maintained independent judicial systems and some of whom retained a third of *galanas* payments for themselves, only moved to adopt English legal process with respect to their Welsh tenants in the late fourteenth or even fifteenth centuries; ethnically English tenants in Wales had always enjoyed a form of English legal process.[8] For example, the Earl of Arundel, lord of Chirk, Bromfield and Yale, Oswestry and Clun in north-east Wales, first issued an amended version of the Statute of Wales in his own name in 1391, while Reginald de Grey, lord of Dyffryn Clwyd, was content to collect a share of at least one *galanas* payment as late as 1430.[9] The long period between the 1284 royal statute and its local adoption throughout Wales was one across which communal legal and financial responsibility associated with the *gwely*, and the very real financial uncertainties which that must have entailed, was replaced by individual responsibility.

The native law of Hywel Dda also prohibited Welsh women from holding land under any circumstance (e.g. ownership, leasehold, dower), prohibited Welshmen from alienating their share of kindred land, and obliged men to employ partible inheritance between male heirs to the fourth degree including bastards.[10] These provisions were intended to preserve the territorial integrity of the *gwely*, so that land would not be lost to the kin group through a female owner's (re)marriage to an outsider, through a woman or man's sale of their share of *gwely* land, or through otherwise unsupported bastards appropriating *gwely* lands, potentially by force. The Statute of Wales changed this by mandating that women in the Principality were to be allowed to inherit in the absence of legitimate male heirs within four degrees, and to have a reasonable dower – a widow's share typically equating to a third of the marital estate – with which to support themselves in the event of their husband's death.[11]

Chapters XII and XIII of the Statute of Wales, dealing with dower and inheritance, are of unparalleled importance to the economic liberation of native Welsh women. To be endowed with property represented a form of economic freedom, potentially sparing never-married adult heiresses the need to be supported by their birth family before marriage, and sparing widows the need to be supported by their birth family or children.[12] Once Welsh women could possess, sell and devise land freely, as well as transfer it through marital union to the control of a different *gwely*, they de facto had the power to break up the territorial integrity, and undermine the economic viability, of *gwelyau*. The cessation of the recognition of bastards' right of inheritance both reduced the number of heirs, in the complete absence of whom the Crown would escheat a deceased man's share of his *gwely*, and increased the possibility of female inheritance. Either outcome compromised the *gwely*. At the same time, it created potential for the illicit alienation of lands to illegitimate heirs, or the violent annexation of lands by such 'disinherited' men. As with the abolition of *galanas*, the 1284 Statute of Wales, in theory, changed property law with immediate effect in the Principality, but widespread acceptance came considerably later. In practice, in the early fourteenth century Welshmen of the Principality might still demand inquiry 'whether they ought to divide their lands with the heirs of a woman or not', and marcher lords proved, if anything, more reluctant to adopt native Welsh women's property rights than they had the abolition of *galanas*.[13] The Earl of Arundel's 1391 customised version of the Statute of Wales, granted to his Welsh tenants of Bromfield and Yale, 'proclaimed starkly' that Welsh women ought not to have these rights of ownership or dower regarding lands by Welsh tenure.[14] Welsh women's property rights were finally adopted in Oswestry lordship by seigniorial charter in 1429, while in the Grey lordship of Dyffryn Clwyd fifteenth-century Welsh women increasingly inherited land, but such inheritances could still be overturned by male complaint as late as 1470, and probably until the Act of Union of 1536.[15]

At the same time, however, the 1284 Statute of Wales retained the dual principles of partible inheritance and the inalienability of Welsh land among native persons, and further reaffirmed them with supplementary ordinances in 1295.[16] This allowed Edward I both to position himself as a defender of Welsh custom in the Principality, and, intentionally or not, to subvert the accumulation of significant wealth in the hands of more prominent Welshmen whose families might in turn grow generationally to wield political influence contrary to the Crown's interest. Marcher lords too retained partible inheritance and prohibited the alienation of lands by Welsh tenure. Yet, as *gwelyau* began slowly to crumble in the fourteenth century through escheat, female inheritance, and increasingly abandonment (see below), Welsh tenure was more and more seen as disadvantageous in comparison to English tenure.

Holdings by English tenure could be engrossed, geographically rationalised and devised to a single heir, thereby concentrating wealth. The same was not true of holdings by Welsh tenure that were increasingly morcellated and scattered. Aspirational Welshmen saw the problems associated with the collapse of the *gwely*, partible inheritance, and the inalienability of Welsh lands at an early stage, unsuccessfully petitioning the Crown for relief from inalienability in the Principality as early at 1307, and securing the grant of a one-off three-year period during which they could alienate land to other free Welshmen at the height of the Great Famine in 1316.[17] Afterwards, the Crown began to collect lucrative fines from Welshmen of the Principality seeking to alienate lands, but declined to lift the general prohibition against alienation until 1507, and even then it was lifted only in the counties of Anglesey, Caernarfon and Meirionnydd.[18] The remainder of the Principality, and the March, would have to wait until the 1536 Act of Union for relief. The long-term problem posed by the twin pillars of inalienability and partible inheritance gave rise in the later-fourteenth and fifteenth centuries to the intensive use of *prid*, or renewable four-year Welsh lease, by which small parcels could be geographically rationalised, albeit temporarily.[19] *Prid* would also emerge as an important means of securing credit against Welsh land, to raise capital, as land could not be sold to do so.[20]

A more permanent solution was for Welshmen to seek to pay a fine to hold their lands by English tenure, or even to have their own legal status reassigned from Welsh to English. One method of changing legal ethnic status was to petition the crown, as Gwilyn ap Gwilym ap Gruffudd did in 1439, asking to be 'made English'.[21] Innumerably more Welshmen, especially in marcher lordships, achieved this change in status by simply buying English legal status – a practice known in Dyffryn Clwyd from at least 1350 – or buying property in a town to attain burgess status (see Chapter 2, Urbanisation and immigration).[22] Burgesses in most towns, such as Ruthin (Denbighshire), were automatically allotted English status, allowing them to hold land by English tenure and securing for them certain advantages at law routinely enjoyed by English colonists, such as judgement in default against absentee Welsh defendants.[23] Such changes of tenure and personal status from Welsh to English, and the public visibility of the benefits of doing so, as demonstrated in lordship courts, would have undermined not only the territorial and economic foundations of *gwelyau*, but also the perceived value of *gwely* membership.

Other elements too were corrosive to the long-term survival of the *gwely*. Famine came to Wales, like the rest of Britain, in the form of combined harvest failure in 1315–17 and cattle murrain in 1319–22, leading to starvation and social dislocation, with its effects being particularly acute in upland areas.[24] Towns, offering lands by privileged burgage tenure, attracted both desperate and aspirational Welsh kinsmen away from their holdings, and furnished a pool of prosperous buyers of vacant Welsh lands.[25] The Black Death, first arriving via the lower Severn valley by March 1349, then precipitated a crisis of a different sort, as *gwelyau* that paid fixed communal taxes were depopulated to such an extent that the survivors could not possibly pay their traditional renders.[26] Antony Carr identified, for example, entire Anglesey *gwelyau* reduced to a single tenant, and many lands there escheated to the Crown.[27] In William Rees's words, social cleavage between tribesmen and non-tribesmen based upon descent, was now giving place to an economic distinction. Greater inequality existed even among landholders themselves, while the landless class was on the increase . . . leaving the 'Welshries' in search of work.[28]

Welsh communities retained a uniquely heightened sense of the importance of kinship with respect to land holding. But, by the second decade of the fourteenth century, 'many of the premier Welsh families' were adopting English inheritance practices, including Owain Glyndŵr's forebears.[29] By the end of the Middle Ages, more prosperous Welshmen would take for granted the capacity to achieve individual proprietorship through the use of *prid*, licences both to alienate hereditary land and to buy land by English tenure, or the purchase of English status.[30] The fourteenth century witnessed the rise of a 'squirearchy' in Wales, that is, of prominent family dynasties that accumulated land and administrative offices to the disparagement of their wider kindred (see below, especially 'After Glyndŵr').[31] The single-tenant farm progressively replaced the *gwely* as the basic economic unit of Welsh agriculture even in almost exclusively Welsh areas. For example, David Longley's detailed study of the two south-western commotes of medieval Anglesey has revealed a 'pattern . . . of increasing consolidation of holdings and the amalgamation of individual small tenancies, with large properties in the hands of a small number of landowners'.[32] Native enclosure of open fields with banks had begun at Vaynol, near St Asaph's, by 1350, and was well advanced on Anglesey by the sixteenth century.[33]

Challenges to the Englishries

The Englishries of Wales also suffered from the catastrophic effects of famine and plague. It is estimated that the Great Famine resulted, directly or indirectly, in the death of 15 per cent of the population of England, with a similar effect on Wales.[34] Wheat and oat prices in the lordship of Dyffryn Clwyd, for example, remained above the crisis thresholds indicative of increased mortality – 7s. and 3s. 3d per quarter respectively – throughout most of the 1315–22 period, peaking in 1315–17 at 14s. to 16s. per quarter of wheat and 7s. to 11s. per quarter of oats.[35] The loss of livestock in the cattle murrain of 1319–22, perhaps killing half or more of the animals that ploughed the fields and provided peasant cultivators with protein in dairy and meat, would have been devastating in upland and lowland areas alike.[36]

Yet it was the Black Death, rather than famine and cattle murrain, that was permanently to alter lowland economic structures. Thus, it is a great shame that no modern, systematic study of the Black Death in Wales has yet been undertaken. Estimates of plague mortality are notoriously difficult, principally because historians must make estimates from the proxy data such as clerical mortality, fallen rents, and inheritance taxes, but a death-rate of at least a third of the population is generally accepted for the first outbreak of plague, and suits the limited Welsh data.[37] The main impact of the plague was to break up patterns of communal agriculture centred on the nucleated villages and on the manors that had been carved out of lowland areas by incoming Anglo-Norman conquerors, and to encourage individual property accumulation. Moreover, this individualism would begin with the effective end of the onerous form of unfree personal status that had come to Wales with the conquerors, especially to the south-east, as peasants sought to renegotiate their rights in the light of lords' new-found desperation to keep their fields tilled. Indeed, as Philip Ziegler poignantly observed in his classic study of the plague: 'In Wales, the Black Death accomplished in a year or two a revolution which in England was worked out over the whole of the fourteenth century.'[38] At Caldicot manor, mid-way between Chepstow and Newport, exceptional mortality meant that by 1362 only 4 of 40 unfree tenants remained alive to perform a paltry 114 of 2,000 days of labour the lord relied upon to maintain and to farm his lands.[39] Landlords were forced to rethink how to generate revenue from their lands as surviving unfree peasants fled or were manumitted.[40] In the Englishry, as in the post-plague Welshry, those entrepreneurial peasants with capital were able to purchase vacant holdings, to enrich themselves, and to enter the emergent squirearchy of Wales.

'The castle', embodying the lord's interests, also saw its economic fortunes transformed. The marcher lords of Wales progressively gave up on attempting to manage directly the cultivation of the demesne lands that they had retained at the conquest and engrossed thereafter for their profit and the provision of their households. Historians of France and England, working with a relative abundance of data, have outlined a scenario in which population decline from 1348–9 coincided with an almost immediate and radical rise in the cost of the now scarce labour required to farm demesne lands increasingly devoid of unfree tenants owing labour service, and an eventual but irresistible reduction in the value of foodstuffs from the 1370s.[41] The challenging, but achievable, task of systematically reconstructing wage and price data from post-plague Wales has not yet been undertaken. Rees collected some indicative data from south Wales, and Carr a smattering of observations from Anglesey, which we may complement here with some north-east Wales data from the lordship of Dyffryn Clwyd.[42]

In general, these data support the notion that labourers' wages in Wales rose sharply after the plague, although wages likely did not double as they did in some instances in France or England.[43] Rees's limited survey suggests that in south Wales fourteenth-century agricultural labourers' daily wages rose from about 2d before the plague to about 3d after it, while Carr found comparable wage rates on Anglesey; these are similar, if slightly lower, than recent estimates of English agricultural labourers' pay.[44] South Wales artisans' daily wages rose from about 3d to about 4.5d, with Anglesey wages perhaps slightly better and English artisans' wages being similar.[45] The flood of post-conquest royal spending in the Principality, as various castles and infrastructures were created, had already pushed up wages and inspired Edward I to issue a 'Statute of Stipends' in royally controlled Wales some time before 1302–3, instituting a form of wage control.[46] But there is only sparse evidence of its enforcement until wages rose after the plague, by which time the Statute of Labourers had been enacted in England, in a parallel and ultimately unsuccessful attempt to curb wage rises there.[47] It is difficult to know how widespread wage controls were in marcher lordships. Something akin to the Statute of Stipends existed in the lordship of Cemaes (Pembrokeshire), while in the lordship of Dyffryn Clwyd, in a 1373 crackdown on what the lord saw as demands for excessive wages, some 217 labourers were fined £8 15s. 2d (about 10d each).[48] The overall picture is one of wages that rose by the latter decades of the fourteenth century to about 150 per cent of pre-plague levels, and of a lordly class sourly inconvenienced by that increase. However, it is important also to recognise that for most persons, apart from artisans, wage labour formed only a small part of their annual income as they continued to toil primarily on their own smallholdings to produce agricultural produce for home consumption and the market.[49] Also, the modest 14 per cent or less of Wales that is croppable limited opportunities for the most common forms of paid labour, like sowing, weeding, reaping, threshing and winnowing grains.[50]

There is less evidence to support the proposition that, as in France and England, higher wages coincided in Wales with a sustained reduction in the value of agricultural goods, especially grains, from the 1370s to the end of the fifteenth century, elevating standards of living for peasants and impoverishing lords.[51] In England, following a long pre- to post-plague trend of rising prices peaking in 1360–9, the value of wheat fell by 25 to 30 per cent from the later 1370s, from over 8s. per quarter to 6s. or less per quarter, although the value of livestock, such as oxen, saw relative long-term stability.[52] Rees, sampling records from south Wales, found that the price per quarter of wheat and oats had risen steadily from the late thirteenth century to the mid-fourteenth century, from about 5s. (wheat) and 2s. (oats) per quarter to more than 7s.6d (wheat) and 2s.6d (oats).[53] These latter values are more-or-less the same as wheat and oat prices in the north Wales lordship of Dyffryn Clwyd in the mid-1320s.[54] But the modest evidence available does not clearly indicate a sustained decline in Welsh grain values in the later fourteenth century. In south Wales the value of wheat fell no lower than 6s. and the value of oats fell no lower than 2s.1d per quarter, a reduction of no more than 20 per cent.[55] And in Dyffryn Clwyd, wheat and oat values remained high in the 1390s, averaging 7s.8d and 2s.8d per quarter, respectively.[56] If Wales experienced either no sustained reduction, or a more limited reduction, of grain prices from the 1370s, when compared to England, then any corresponding improvements to standards of living for peasants would have been more muted in Wales. Livestock prices in Wales, as in England, remained strong or increased slightly across the fourteenth and fifteenth centuries. The value of a cow in Dyffryn Clwyd, for example, rose from about 6s. in the 1330s to about 6s.8d by the 1390s, with the more variable value of an ox being about 10s. to 12s. throughout the period.[57] Stable cattle prices may have been particularly beneficial to the pastoral sector of the Welsh economy, so important to the tenantry of predominantly upland lordships such as Brecon and cattle-droving towns such as Cowbridge (Glamorgan).[58]

Was the 'long fifteenth century' in Wales, from the 1370s, a 'Golden Age' of the labourer at the expense of the lordly class, as has been asserted of England?[59] It was not. Wages rose, benefiting labours such as harvest workers while disproportionately and adversely impacting the profitability of demesne agriculture, but opportunities for work were limited by the modest extent of arable agriculture in Wales, and grain prices remained relatively high. Moreover, the powerful role of judicial lordship and arbitrary taxation in Wales would expose peasants to offsetting exploitation (see Chapter 2, Lordship and society, and below), and the coming of the Glyndŵr rebellion from 1400 would serve to cripple the rural economy for a century.

Given the modest post-plague reduction in the value of agricultural produce in Wales, it was depopulation itself, first and foremost, that led most substantially to the subsequent unprofitability of demesne agriculture, and drove lords to seek other ways of extracting revenues from the land and remaining populace. Rees Davies, in a study of south-east Wales where unfree tenants were relatively numerous before the plague, found that demesne direct management was abandoned at Caldicot in 1362, at Monmouth and much of the lordship of Usk in the 1360s and on manors in Newport in the 1380s.[60] The total revenue of Usk, for example, fell from £1,192 in 1300 to £467 in 1398, as lords became 'poorly remunerated stockholders in the soil'.[61]

The crown was almost exclusively an absentee landlord in Wales, and, by the latter half of the fourteenth century, so too were most marcher lords. Direct oversight of demesne agriculture was abandoned in favour of leasing the king's or the marcher lords' lands for increasingly lengthy terms in order to hedge against falling revenues.[62] When a cycle of economic decay began in the later fourteenth century an increasingly regressive economic exploitation of the populace also began. As James Given observed, conquest in Wales resulted in 'more effective techniques for mobilizing the resources of its subjects... but also removed from the scene any... authority that might have been able to resist and moderate' those demands.[63]

Historians of Britain and Europe have long argued that the first decades after the Black Death saw a 'seigniorial reaction', in which landlords sought to battle falling revenues by imposing a harsh 'neo-serfdom', subverting the free operation of land and labour markets to their own gain.[64] Equally, the final decades of the fourteenth century – the 1381 Peasants' Revolt being a dividing line in England – are thought to have seen an empowered peasantry cast off the lingering vestiges of overbearing lordship, attain improved tenures and lower rents, and expose themselves more directly to the mixed prospects of a more market-orientated economy.[65] Some short-term seigniorial reactions to changed economic conditions, such as the attempted enforcement of wage controls discussed above, existed in Wales. Rents fell on Anglesey and some south Wales manors from the 1370s, and serfdom and customary tenure declined rapidly in Wales, with Chirk lordship receiving a 1355 charter confirming freemen in their bond lands, while similar provision was made at White Castle (Monmouthshire) by 1386 and later at Ogmore (Glamorgan); at Dyffryn Clwyd the number of unfree in the main grain-growing areas of the lordship had fallen from 212 to 47 by 1381.[66] Across Wales, those with capital to hand had improved their position by engrossing their holdings with those of their deceased neighbours, free and unfree, or by re-entering abandoned lands under improved free tenure. But while the liberation of the unfree, and the reduction of financial exploitation that it would seem to imply, was arguably a revolution in the intensively cropped heartlands of champion England, it was of much more limited importance in Wales. Serfdom in Wales was focused on the old princely demesne lands of the north-west, the heavily colonised south-east and certain Englishries, and it was relatively light where it existed among the Welsh.[67] For most marcher lords and their tenants, rents had long been less important than the economics of judicial lordship and arbitrary taxation (see Chapter 2, Lordship and society, and below). For example, at Chirk the lord attempted to offset falling revenues by inventing, in 1390–1, a £500 community fine for failing to carry timber – a moribund obligation, just the latest in a series of fines – at a time when annual rents did not much exceed £150.[68] And the most significant social and economic fault line had never been that separating free and unfree, but that separating English and Welsh, the latter of which tended more often to be subject to the caprices of marcher lordship (see below).

In Wales the key seigniorial response to falling revenues was not the manipulation of land and labour markets but an intensification of non-rent-based income generation that, while interrupted by the Glyndŵr rebellion and gradually to lose its potency, would linger until the sixteenth-century Act of Union. The main regressive form of revenue raising was the 'farming' of offices such as parker, forester, manager of the lord's mill(s) or bailiff, in which the right to exercise certain plenary powers of the lord, for a set period of time, was auctioned to the highest bidder, the lessee taking as profit all receipts beyond the sum promised to the lord. At Chirk, for instance, the value of the farm of mills, tolls and offices quadrupled from £40 annually in 1322–3 to £177 in 1378–9, about the same as all lordship rents.[69] The most contentious revenue stream put to farm was the ethnically specific *amobr*, or Welsh virginity tax, which officious farmers expanded from a one-time payment made by a maiden's family at her marriage, to a heavy and recurrent penalty due at marriage and each known instance of sex outside wedlock.[70] This innovation had its roots in the pre-plague period. Edward II was compelled to respond to aggrieved petitioners of the royal Principality as early as 1316, issuing an ordinance to offer them 'relief from the superabundance of bailiffs in those parts' with respect to the collection of certain dues.[71] Nevertheless, farming became widespread in the first decades of the fourteenth century and intensified after the Black Death, increasing tenants' financial burdens while, in the long term, lords' net incomes nevertheless continued to fall largely owing to their own officials' neglect and fraud, leading cyclically to yet further attempts at decreasingly effective revenue-raising exploitation.[72]

Townspeople too experienced the economic impacts of famine and plague. Famine years may actually have expanded towns as paupers arrived in search of food.[73] Similarly, just after the plague, vacant tenements that offered economic privileges could quickly be filled. Nevertheless, in the long term, a cessation of immigration from England, where land was now more abundantly available, and a steadily contracting customer base were less easily surmountable problems. The period following the Black Death of 1348–9 would see what Ralph Griffiths has called a 'winnowing' of the hundred or so towns of Wales, as weaker foundations failed and a reordering of the urban hierarchy took place.[74] The alarmed reaction of townsmen was to discourage competition, along ethnic lines where expedient, by challenging the right of Welsh men and women to enjoy borough liberties.[75] While Edward I had, some time between 1284 and 1295, proclaimed that the burgesses of his new boroughs in north Wales should be English, this had almost never been the case in practice.[76] Yet, in the decades after the Black Death, this disused edict was dredged up and applied haphazardly in towns, such as Harlech (Merionethshire) and Cricieth (Caernarfonshire), where Welsh burgesses were in a minority.[77] In Hope (Flintshire), hardly two years after the plague, the town's English burgesses sought, and were granted by Edward III in 1351, a new borough charter specifically excluding Welsh burgesses, whose property seems to have been confiscated.[78] A similar action was undertaken by the English of Flint (Flintshire) who received a new charter in 1360.[78]

Such incidents, though probably confined to a minority of boroughs, contributed to a sense of oppression and discrimination, exacerbating the Anglo-Welsh tensions arising from the imposition of ethnic-specific taxes such as *amobr*. Moreover, they took place against the backdrop of 'a major redistribution of wealth, mainly, but by no means exclusively, in the interests of the more fortunate of the gentry and the better-off tenants', that is to say, the rise of the squirearchy.[80] Towns were alien-created institutions that were now the sites of selective but highly visible episodes of ethnic discrimination, and were repositories of material wealth in a countryside riven by increasing inequalities of wealth. It is therefore unsurprising that during the course of the revolt of Owain Glyndŵr, which would devastate the country's ailing economic base, more than forty towns were sacked or attacked and in some instances burned, irrespective of the ethnicity of their occupants.[81] Glyndŵr's sacking and burning of Ruthin on 18 September 1400, where half the inhabitants were Welsh, in the lordship of Dyffryn Clwyd, marked the beginning of the revolt. A century later, many ravaged towns, such as Overton (Flintshire) or Dinefwr (Carmarthenshire), remained nearly unoccupied or were wholly desolate and never to recover.[82]

Parts of the nascent urban network of Wales also suffered from other long-term problems, which were only exacerbated by Glyndŵr's attacks. Many towns had been founded in defensible hilltop positions that were poorly suited to peacetime trade, such as Dolforwyn (Montgomeryshire), which had already failed by Glyndŵr's time, and Denbigh (Denbighshire), which ultimately prospered but would move its focus to the foot of the hill beneath the castle.[83] Others suffered from natural degradation, such as Kenfig (Glamorgan), a twelfth-century Norman foundation with a population of about 600–700 in 1307, but which had been virtually abandoned by 1470 owing to inundation by sand dunes.[84] Meanwhile, at Kidwelly (Carmarthenshire), another Norman foundation, silt and sand so clogged the mouth of the River Gwendraeth Fach by the fifteenth century that larger ships could no longer land at the town, making recovery impossible after destruction by Glyndŵr's rebels in 1403.[85]

The first decades of the fifteenth century saw England, and Europe, spiral into the so-called 'European depression' of the fifteenth century. The causes were complex, but the main ones were the long-term effects of depopulation, the exhaustion of European silver mines, which meant shortages of bullion for coin production, and the disruption caused by the latter phase of the Hundred Years' War, which ended in 1453 with England's loss of virtually all of her French possessions.[86] The depression meant that Wales, which conducted virtually all of its trade with England, had little hope of economic reconstruction following the ravages of the Glyndŵr revolt. Organised Welsh resistance ended, in the main, with the English recapture of Aberystwyth and Harlech in 1409, but continued in remote localities well past Glyndŵr's disappearance in 1415 and ultimately blurred into economically crippling endemic brigandage that would continue throughout the fifteenth century.[87]

After Glyndŵr

The response of the English government to plague and rebellion in Wales brought its own problems. Following the plague of 1348-9, the 1353 Statute of the Staple streamlined the staple system and New Carmarthen became the only staple port in Wales, leaving north Wales without a staple, although merchants of Wales were authorised to bring their goods to English staples, such as Bristol.[88] Ports in marcher lordships remained outside royal control, but in 1441-2 a statute was introduced making staple goods passing through Welsh ports *en route* to or from England (to take advantage of preferable tax rates, see above, Chapter 2, Industry and commerce), liable to confiscation at the English border.[89] This was problematic for the port of Chepstow, in particular, hard by the border.[90]

Between 1401 and 1402, in response to revolt, Henry IV's parliament introduced no less than fifteen penal measures against the Welsh.[91] One allowed English merchants and peasants whose goods had been stolen by those dwelling in marcher lordships to demand restitution from the relevant lordship and, if restitution was not forthcoming within seven days – a wholly unrealistic timeframe – to confiscate goods arriving from Wales sufficient to cover their losses plus expenses.[92] Other measures attempted to ban Welshmen from purchasing property in the royal boroughs of Wales, thereby stifling needed investment for recovery, and to stop the Welsh congregating in one place, which would surely have been necessary for trade as much as insurrection.[93] Moreover, these penal measures were confirmed by statute in 1446-7, indicating at least some will to attempt their enforcement over several decades.[94]

The years after the Glyndŵr rebellion thus saw a continuation, or even intensification, of economic developments that were already in train before 1400. Seigniorial profits continued to plummet in most marcher lordships, even though the intensive farming of offices continued. The revenues of the south-eastern lordship of Newport, Gwent, far away from the revolt's Snowdonia epicentre, declined by 10 per cent between 1400 and 1447; the revenues of the ravaged lordship of Denbigh, nearer the threshold of Snowdonia, declined from £1,000 in 1400 to just £50 in 1500.[95] Widespread confiscations of property following the Glyndŵr rebellion, especially in north-east Wales, provided a second opportunity, like that following the Black Death, for those with wealth to engross their holdings with those of the dead or disinherited.[96] In the Dyffryn Clwyd commote of Llannerch alone, at least 117 leases of vacant land were issued between 1410 and 1422.[97] The *gwely* all but disappeared, as did the despised institution of unfree status, marking a pronounced shift from communal to individual economic responsibility. The discrete smallholding based on the nuclear family became the default peasant agrarian unit, eventually rendering economic distinctions between the 'Englishry' and 'Welshry' largely meaningless.[98] In order to attract new tenants to vacant holdings, lands formerly subject to Welsh or customary tenure were offered at free English tenure, irrespective of the new tenant's ethnicity.[99] Carr has carefully reconstructed the process of estate engrossment and wealth stratification on Anglesey.[100] As in England, this may have reduced the net imbalance of power and wealth between landlords and peasants, but Wales remained a place both relatively impoverished by English standards and of local 'haves' and 'have nots'.[101] Richer peasants and members of the privileged squirearchy – whom Davies identified as having a landed income of just £10, or half an English knight's fee, in view of the relative poverty of Wales – worked to engross their holdings by acquiring the lands of their less fortunate neighbours.[102] Between 1420 and 1453, for example, Bartholomew Bolde of Conwy acquired hundreds of freehold properties from peasants in the Conwy valley.[103] This process focused in the squirearchy's hands the modest profits of the many smallholdings that they accrued, allowing them to achieve locally notable prosperity. The squirearchy, working to distinguish itself from less fortunate landholders, formed close bonds across Anglo-Welsh lines, culturally assimilating, intermarrying and acting as patrons of Welsh poetry, as the Hanmers of Maelor Saesneg (Flintshire), Stradlings of St Donat's (Glamorgan) and many others did.[104]

The fruits of the squirearchy's fifteenth-century accomplishments in personal enrichment were manifest in 'one of the great ages of Welsh vernacular architecture', even as the Welsh economy languished in a decades-long post-Glyndŵr economic depression.[105] The lesser of them constructed, especially in eastern Wales, a large number of well-built, undefended farm houses, indistinguishable from those found in many English shires.[106] The greater of them constructed, in the south-west of Wales, first-floor halls of stone, such as Eastington, Rhoscrowther (Pembrokeshire), occupied by the Perrot family who later moved to Carew Castle.[107] In northern and eastern Wales they constructed great hall-houses of wood, such as Hafoty House, Llansadwrn (Anglesey), built by the Norres family before passing to the Bulkeleys in 1511, the latter family already possessing a hall-house called Henblas that they had built in Beaumaris in 1475.[108]

It is in marked contrast to the squirearchy's growing fifteenth-century prosperity that the wider Welsh economy remained stagnant. Only the cloth industry escaped the general post-Glyndŵr economic recession, with a guild of fullers and weavers – unique to Wales in so far as we know – founded at Ruthin in 1447.[109] The fifteenth-century cloth industry, like the more ancient cattle trade of Wales, looked east for its markets. Griffiths has set out with clarity the importance of Welsh cloth and cattle trade to the post-Glyndŵr recovery of Chester, Shrewsbury, Hereford, Gloucester and Bristol, along with the importance of Welsh immigration to England.[110] Shrewsbury was so keen to monopolise the Welsh cloth trade that in 1470 an ordinance was passed prohibiting the town's drapers purchasing Welsh cloth through middlemen based in Oswestry, Welshpool or anywhere else in the March, in order to ensure that borough traders would only buy Welsh cloth directly from producers.[111] Immigration was so considerable that, at Hereford, from 1450, the labouring class of the city was occasionally referred to in times of civic infighting as 'the Welsh', while city officials and court litigants with Welsh names crop up in fifteenth-century records produced along the length of the border.[112] Bristol, in particular, as England's third-largest city with about 8,000 souls, experienced exceptional Welsh immigration, with successful merchant Henry Vaughan, who was probably of Cardiganshire stock, serving as mayor when in May 1486 the city was visited by the first Tudor king, Henry VII, who had the previous year made much capital of his Welsh ancestry in attaining native support for his invasion and conquest of England.[113]

Maritime trade meant that south Wales was better connected to the English economy than other parts of Wales, benefiting the area from Pembrokeshire to Monmouthshire.[114] At Bristol, in the late fifteenth century, ships from Tenby, Chepstow, Haverfordwest, Milford Haven and elsewhere in Wales landed goods from as far afield as Ireland, France, Spain and Portugal, at a quay that became known as 'Welsh Back'.[115] By 1532–52, some 15 per cent of Bristol apprentices, 483 men and women in all, were from Wales, over 80 per cent of whom were from the southern counties and lordships of Wales.[116] Ultimately, the involvement of the ports of south Wales in trade with England would allow them, along with their hinterlands, to emerge as economic leaders in the Tudor era, and, indeed, to maintain their relative prosperity for centuries to come.[117] Meanwhile, depopulated and disorderly inland rural areas, especially upland Wales, languished in persistent poverty, presided over by the new squirearchy, until at least the seventeenth century.[118]

At the end of the Middle Ages, when Henry VIII brought about the Act of Union of England and Wales of 1536, the Welsh economy was more intimately linked to the English economy than ever before. The agricultural interior of Wales was impoverished. The flow of immigration to Wales from England before the Black Death of 1348–9 was reversed from at least the mid-fifteenth century, with increasing numbers of Welsh now moving to England in search of education and work. Only the cloth-producing areas, especially in the northern March, and the port towns of the south Wales coast exhibited signs of durable, if modest, prosperity as they benefited from the recovery of the English economy under Tudor rule. The Welsh economy would have to await early modern industrialisation to see widespread and sustained growth.

Notes

1. D. H. Owen, 'The Englishry of Denbigh: An English Colony in Medieval Wales', *TransCymm*. (1974/5), 57–76.
2. See A. D. Carr, 'Wales: economy and society', in S. H. Rigby (ed.), *A Companion to Britain in the Later Middle Ages* (Oxford, 2003), pp. 125–41; *LordSoc.*, pp. 406–10.
3. For the text of the statute see *Statutes*, pp. 2–27.
4. Ll. B. Smith, 'The Statute of Wales, 1284', *WHR*, 10 (1980–1), 134; *Statutes*, p. 2.
5. T. G. Watkin, *The Legal History of Wales*, 2nd edn (Cardiff, 2012), p. 67; R. R. Davies, 'The Survival of the Bloodfeud in Medieval Wales', *History*, 54 (1969), 338–57.
6. Ll. B. Smith, 'A Contribution to the History of *Galanas* in Late-medieval Wales', *Studia Celtica*, 43 (2009), 87–94; Davies, 'The Survival', 346. See below for cattle values.
7. Smith, 'A Contribution', 87.
8. Smith, 'A Contribution', 87–8; *Statutes*, pp. 8–9.
9. Smith, 'A Contribution', 87–8; Smith, 'The Statute of Wales', 135.
10. Ll. B. Smith, 'Towards a history of women in late medieval Wales', in M. Roberts and S. Clarke (eds), *Women and Gender in Early Modern Wales* (Cardiff, 2000), pp. 19–20; On the use of Welsh lease to avoid alienation, see Ll. B. Smith, '*Tir Prid*: Deeds of Gage of Land in Late-medieval Wales', *BBCS*, 27 (1977), 263–77.
11. Smith, 'Towards a history', p. 21; *Statutes*, pp. 24–5.
12. D. Jenkins, 'Property interests in the classical Welsh law of women', in D. Jenkins and M. E. Owen (eds), *The Welsh Law of Women* (Cardiff, 1980), pp. 71–2, 85–6.

13 Smith, 'Towards a history', pp. 21–2.
14 Smith, 'Towards a history', p. 21.
15 Smith, 'Towards a history', p. 22.
16 Ll. B. Smith, 'The Gage and the Land Market in Medieval Wales', *EcHR*, 29 (1976), 540–1; H. Ellis (ed.), *Registrum Vulgariter Nuncupatum: The Record of Caernarvon* (London, 1838), p. 132.
17 J. B. Smith, 'Crown and Community in the Principality of North Wales in the Reign of Henry Tudor', *WHR*, 3 (1966), 146–8.
18 Smith, 'Crown and Community', 150–1; Smith, 'The Gage and the Land Market', 541.
19 Smith, '*Tir Prid*: Deeds of Gage', 263–77.
20 Smith, 'The Gage and the Land Market', 548–9.
21 Smith, 'Crown and Community', 151.
22 Purchase of English status, Ruthin 1350, TNA, SC 2/218/1 m.7; E. A. Lewis, *The Medieval Boroughs of Snowdonia* (London, 1912), p. 256.
23 English status as burgess, Ruthin 1394, creditor Ieuan ap Dafydd Fychan, legal Englishman, versus absentee debtor and legal Welshman Gwillym ap Dafydd ap Gruffydd. TNA, PRO, SC 2/220/9, m.13d.
24 M. F. Stevens, 'The Great Famine in Dyffryn Clwyd, 1315–22', *DHST*, 63 (2015), 13–35.
25 *LordSoc.*, pp. 411–12; M. F. Stevens, 'Anglo-Welsh towns of the early fourteenth century: a survey of urban origins, property-holding and ethnicity', in *UrbanCult.*, pp. 139–50.
26 W. Rees, 'The Black Death in Wales', *TransRoyal*, 4th series, 3 (1920), 117–19.
27 A. D. Carr, *Medieval Anglesey*, 2nd edn (Llangefni, 2011), p. 122.
28 Rees, 'The Black Death', 134.
29 A. D. M. Barrell and R. R. Davies, 'Land, Lineage, and Revolt in North-east Wales, 1243–1441: A Case Study', *Cambrian Medieval Celtic Studies*, 29 (1995), 44.
30 Smith, 'The Gage and the Land', 550; Ll. B. Smith, 'Family, Land and Inheritance in Late Medieval Wales: A Case Study of Llannerch in the Lordship of Dyffryn Clwyd', *WHR*, 27 (2015), 417–58; Barrell and Davies, 'Land, Lineage, and Revolt', 41–4.
31 *LordSoc.*, pp. 413–424; the *uchelwr*, or 'squirearchy'/'gentry', have been investigated most thoroughly by A. D. Carr, *The Gentry of North Wales in the Later Middle Ages* (Cardiff, 2017).

32   D. Longley, 'Medieval Settlement and Landscape Change on Anglesey', *Landscape History*, 23 (2001), 39. See also, on governance, D. Longley, 'Gwynedd before and after the conquest', in D. M. Williams and J. R. Kenyon (eds), *The Impact of the Edwardian Castles in Wales* (Oxford, 2010), pp. 16–32.
33   National Library of Wales, SA/MISC/196 (Vaynol); Longley, 'Medieval Settlement', 39.
34   I. Kershaw, 'The Great Famine and Agrarian Crisis in England, 1315–1322', *P&P*, 59 (1973), 11; P. R. Schofield, 'Wales and the Great Famine of the Early Fourteenth Century', *WHR*, 29 (2018), 143–67.
35   Stevens, 'The Great Famine', 20–2.
36   Stevens, 'The Great Famine', 25–30; P. Slavin, 'The fifth rider of the apocalypse: the great cattle plague in England and Wales and its economic consequences, 1319–50', in S. Cavaciocchi (ed.), *Le interazioni fra economia e ambiente biologico nell'Europa preindustriale, secc. XIII – XVIII* (Florence, 2010), p. 170 (figure 1).
37   Rees, 'The Black Death', 117–25.
38   P. Ziegler, *The Black Death*, 2nd edn (London, 1998), p. 201.
39   R. R. Davies, 'Plague and revolt', in *GwentCH*, p. 223.
40   *LordSoc.*, pp. 437–43.
41   D. L. Farmer, 'Prices and wages, 1350–1500', in E. Miller (ed.), *AgHist.*, vol. III: *1348–1500* (Cambridge, 1991), pp. 97–135; L. Ridolfi, 'L'histoire immobile? Six Centuries of Real Wages in France from Louis IX to Napoleon III: 1250–1860', *LEM Working Paper Series* (2017/14), www.lem.sssup.it/wplem.html, figures 5–7.
42   *SouthWales*, pp. 263–5; Carr, *Medieval Anglesey*, pp. 87–9.
43   Farmer 'Prices and wages', pp. 436–7, 467–83; Ridolfi, 'L'histoire immobile?', figure 6.
44   *SouthWales*, p. 265; Carr, *Medieval Anglesey*, pp. 87–9; G. Clark, 'The Long March of History: Farm Wages, Population, and Economic Growth, England 1209–1869', *EcHR*, 60 (2007), 99–100, table 1.
45   *SouthWales*, p. 265; Carr, *Medieval Anglesey*, pp. 87–9; Farmer 'Prices and wages', p. 471, table 5.8.
46   *SouthWales*, p. 269, n. 1 (31 E. I).
47   *SouthWales*, p. 269; Farmer 'Prices and wages', pp. 483–90.

48 *LordSoc.*, p. 435.
49 J. Hatcher, 'Unreal wages: long-run living standards and the "Golden Age" of the fifteenth century', in B. Dodds and C. D. Liddy (eds), *Commercial Activity, Markets and Entrepreneurs in the Middle Ages* (Woodbridge, 2011), pp. 1–24.
50 E. Armstrong, 'Research Briefing: The Farming Sector in Wales', *National Assembly for Wales Research Service*, paper 16–053 (2016), 6.
51 Ridolfi has argued that enhanced standards of living were more short-lived in France than England. Ridolfi, 'L'histoire immobile?', esp. figures 5–7.
52 Farmer 'Prices and wages', pp. 433–5.
53 *South Wales*, p. 265.
54 Stevens, 'The Great Famine', 21–2 (figure 1).
55 Farmer 'Prices and Wages', p. 265.
56 TNA, PRO SC 2/220/7 m.15 to SC 2/221/1 m.28d. (18 wheat observations and 10 oat observations).
57 TNA, PRO, SC 2/220/8 m.17 to SC 2/220/10 m.8. (17 cow observations and 15 ox observations).
58 D. Walker, *Medieval Wales* (Cambridge, 1990), pp. 59–61; D. M. Robinson, *Cowbridge: The Archaeology and Topography of a Small Market Town in the Vale of Glamorgan* (Swansea, 1980), pp. 42, 60 (figure 10).
59 For a recent review see C. Dyer, 'A Golden Age rediscovered: labourers' wages in the fifteenth century', in M. Allen and D. Coffman (eds), *Money Prices and Wages: Essays in Honour of Professor Nicholas Mayhew* (Houndmills, 2015), pp. 180–95.
60 Davies, 'Plague and revolt', p. 277.
61 G. Williams, *Renewal and Reformation Wales, c.1415–1642* (Oxford, 1993), p. 79.
62 Williams, *Renewal and Reformation*, pp. 80–1.
63 J. Given, 'The Economic Consequences of the English Conquest of Gwynedd', *Speculum*, 74 (1989), 11–45.
64 For a recent overview and challenge to this orthodoxy see M. Bailey, 'The myth of the "seigniorial reaction" in England after the Black Death', in M. Kowaleski, J. Langdon and P. R. Schofield (eds), *Peasants and Lords in the Medieval English Economy: Essays in Honour of Bruce M. S. Campbell* (Turnhout, 2015), pp. 147–72.

65 The classic peasant liberation narrative is R. H. Hilton, *Bond Men Made Free: Medieval Peasant Movements and the English Rising of 1381* (London, 1973); W. Blockmans and P. Hoppenbrouwers, *Introduction to Medieval Europe, 300–1500*, 2nd edn (London, 2014), pp. 340–3.
66 Carr, *Medieval Anglesey*, pp. 309–12; *SouthWales*, pp. 247–8, 251–2; *LordSoc.*, pp. 437–8.
67 Carr, *Medieval Anglesey*, pp. 91–108; *SouthWales*, pp. 149–76.
68 Ll. B. Smith, 'Seignorial Income in the Fourteenth Century: The Arundels in Chirk', *BBCS*, 28 (1979), 447.
69 Smith, 'Seignorial Income', 446.
70 L. Johnson, '*Amobr* and *Amobrwyr*: The Collection of Marriage Fees and Sexual Fines in Late Medieval Wales', *TransCymm.*, 18 (2012), 10–21; M. F. Stevens, *Urban Assimilation in Post-conquest Wales: Ethnicity, Gender and Economy in Ruthin, 1282–1348* (Cardiff, 2010), pp. 198–9.
71 *SouthWales*, p. 107–8; *LordSoc.*, p. 209–12.
72 Williams, *Renewal and Reformation*, p. 79; Smith, 'Seignorial Income', 450–1.
73 Stevens, 'The Great Famine', 30.
74 R. A. Griffiths, 'Wales and the Marches', in D. Palliser (ed.), *The Cambridge Urban History of Britain*, vol. 1 (Cambridge, 2000), p. 699.
75 M. F. Stevens and R. Czaja, 'The place of native populations in the chartered towns of conquered regions: Wales and Prussia as a comparative case study' (forthcoming).
76 Griffiths, 'Wales and the Marches', pp. 705–6; Stevens, 'Anglo-Welsh towns'. p. 141 (table 6.1); Ellis (ed.), *Record of Caernarvon*, p. 132.
77 Griffiths, 'Wales and the Marches', p. 706.
78 Griffiths, 'Wales and the Marches', p. 706.
79 Griffiths, 'Wales and the Marches', p. 706.
80 Williams, *Renewal and Reformation*, p. 79; *LordSoc.*, pp. 413–24; Carr, *The Gentry*, pp. 67–105.
81 *Towns*, pp. 25–6.
82 *Towns*, p. 26.
83 *Towns*, pp. 121–3, 130–1.
84 *Towns*, pp. 149–51.
85 *Towns*, pp. 152–4; Griffiths, 'Wales and the Marches', p. 702.

86   P. Nightingale, 'England and the European Depression of the Mid-fifteenth Century', *The Journal of European Economic History*, 26 (1997), 631–56.
87   R. R. Davies, *The Revolt of Owain Glyn Dŵr* (Oxford, 1995), p. 125; E. A. Rees, *Welsh Outlaws and Bandits: Political Rebellion and Lawlessness in Wales, 1400–1603* (Kings Norton, 2001), esp. pp. 13–44.
88   *Statutes*, p. 30; E. A. Lewis, 'The Development of Industry and Commerce in Wales During the Middle Ages', *TransRoyal*, new series, 17 (1903), 152–3..
89   *Statutes*, p. 43.
90   S. Dimmock, 'Reassessing the Towns of Southern Wales in the Later Middle Ages', *Urban History*, 32 (2005), 42–4.
91   *Statutes*, pp. xliii–xlvi.
92   *Statutes*, pp. 30–1.
93   *Statutes*, pp. 33–4.
94   *Statutes*, p. 45.
95   Williams, *Renewal and Reformation*, p. 79.
96   Barell and Davies, 'Land, Lineage, and Revolt', 48–9.
97   Barell and Davies, 'Land, Lineage, and Revolt', 49.
98   Carr, *Medieval Anglesey*, p. 123.
99   *LordSoc.*, pp. 441–3.
100 Carr, *Medieval Anglesey*, p. 123–41.
101 R. Britnell, *Britain and Ireland, 1050–1530* (Oxford, 2004), p. 439.
102 *LordSoc.*, p. 413; Carr, *Medieval Anglesey*, pp. 159–84; Carr, *The Gentry*, pp. 67–105 (wealth of the gentry).
103 Britnell, *Britain and Ireland*, p. 445; for a reconstruction see, T. Jones Pierce, 'The gafael in Bangor MS 1939', in *WelshSoc.*, pp. 195–228.
104 *LordSoc.*, p. 419; Carr, *The Gentry*, pp. 157–72 (marriage alliances), 204–35 (cultural patronage).
105 Williams, *Renewal and Reformation*, p. 111.
106 P. Smith, *Houses of the Welsh Countryside: A Study in Historical Geography* (London, 1975), p. 11.
107 Smith, *Houses of the Welsh*, pp. 21–4, 31.
108 Smith, *Houses of the Welsh*, pp., 42, 51; D. Longley, 'Hafoty and its Occupiers', *TransAng.* (2007), 25–39; Carr, *Medieval Anglesey*, pp. 156–7, 176, 203.

109 Stevens, *Urban Assimilation*, p. 248. By comparison, only forty-nine years later in 1496, as the Tudor economy began to recover, was a brotherhood of corvesers and shoemakers established, reflecting Ruthin's other main industry.
110 R. A. Griffiths, 'After Glyn Dŵr: An Age of Reconciliation?', *Proceedings of the British Academy*, 117 (2002), 139–164, esp. 145–55.
111 Griffiths, 'After Glyn Dŵr', 147.
112 Griffiths, 'After Glyn Dŵr', 145–6.
113 Griffiths, 'After Glyn Dŵr', 153–4; Evans, *Wales and the Wars of the Roses*, pp. 119–33.
114 Griffiths, 'Medieval Severnside'.
115 Griffiths, 'After Glyn Dŵr', 152.
116 S. Dimmock, 'The Origins of Welsh Apprentices in Sixteenth-century Bristol', *WHR*, 24 (2008–9), pp. 119–20.
117 P. Fleming, 'The Severn Sea: urban networks and connections in the fifteenth century', in E. T. Jones and R. Stone (eds), *The World of the Newport Medieval Ship: Trade, Politics and Shipping in the Mid-fifteenth Century* (Cardiff, 2018), pp. 116–33.
118 Powell has sought to moderate this view. N. M. W. Powell, '"Near the margin of existence?" Upland Prosperity in Wales during the Early Modern Period', *Studia Celtica*, 41 (2007), 137–62.

Chapter four
MODELLING THE ECONOMY OF MEDIEVAL WALES

RATHER THAN providing a conclusion which simply summarises the developments outlined in the previous chapters, it is more useful to finish this volume with a consideration of how the course of these developments ought to be interpreted. Historians of medieval Britain and Europe have often, whether consciously or not, applied a number of overarching models of economic change. The three most prominent of these 'classic supermodels' are the 'demographic' model, also called the 'population and resources' or 'neo-Malthusian' model; the 'Marxist' or 'neo-Marxist' model, focusing on 'class, power and property relations'; and, finally, the 'commercialisation' model focusing on 'commercialisation, markets and technology'.[1] These 'classic supermodels' have been applied in a number of national contexts and are both supported and burdened by their own extensive historiographies. They have their own strengths and weaknesses, and are not always mutually exclusive. Most helpful for students of Welsh history, each has been set out with respect to Wales's near neighbour England by John Hatcher and Mark Bailey in *Modelling the Middle Ages*.[2] But to what extent do they help us to understand economic change in medieval Wales?

Historians of Wales have rarely engaged in theoretical discussion of the economy, but they do implicitly focus on particular causal factors aligned to one historical tradition or another, as outlined in this book's Introduction. For example, Antony Carr's assertion that 'the primary cause of economic change in Wales was the rise in population ... between 1050 and 1300' expresses an adherence to the demographic model.[3] Yet, Carr is unusual in taking such a clear position. Historians of Wales have looked at a variety of topics, such as population, personal freedom and urbanisation, which can inform broader, more theoretical interpretations of change, but the paucity of discussion regarding Wales means that conclusions arrived at by applying theoretical models of change to the English evidence are routinely extended to Wales (see Introduction). This happens despite fundamental differences between the geography, society and governance of Wales and England. This chapter briefly sets out the main elements of the three most well-known models, and assesses their applicability to Wales. This discussion is intended only to be indicative, not exhaustive, pointing the way for further research.

The demographic model

The demographic model is based on the assumption that the main driver of economic change in pre-industrial society was the rise and fall of population. It is contended that the 'British Isles' had, given contemporary levels of agricultural output, a maximum sustainable population at any point in time. Associated with Thomas Robert Malthus, by way of his 1798 work *An Essay on the Principle of Population*, and elaborated in dialogue with David Ricardo over the first two decades of the nineteenth century, this model supposes that the number of people in a resource-rich land will increase in number exponentially (or 'geometrically', for example, 2, 4, 8, 16, 32, etc.), while food production only increases arithmetically (for example, 2, 4, 6, 8, 10, etc.).[4] As a consequence, periodic overpopulation will result, giving rise to 'positive checks', such as famine or disease, that reduce the population by increased mortality, thereby freeing up resources and so making possible a new cycle of population increase. 'Preventative checks' on population growth, such as abstinence or delayed marriage resulting from increasing poverty due to overpopulation, are perceived to be generally ineffective or inadequate in an age lacking effective contraception. As applied to medieval England, it is contended that the population trebled between the Norman invasion of 1066 and *c*.1300, rising from around two million to about six million.[5] This resulted in increasing hardship by the last decades of the thirteenth century as food prices and rents rose and real wages fell, and ultimately the Great Famine of 1315–22, a pan-European climate-influenced arable food-production crisis and concomitant cattle murrain, in which as much as 15 per cent of the English population perished.[6] Moreover, Philip Slavin has argued that famine created a nutritionally vulnerable population, living in a still densely settled landscape, who were structurally predisposed to exceptional mortality of at least 33 per cent during the Black Death of 1348–9.[7]

This demographic model sees the economic expansion experienced across Western Europe between the eleventh and fourteenth centuries as a function of population growth, and the pan-European economic depression of the fifteenth century as primarily a function of plague-induced population collapse. Moreover, a host of socioeconomic consequences are attributed to the radical restructuring of land-labour relations resulting from this depopulation with a shift from a situation of land shortage and labour surplus to one of land abundance and labour shortage being seen as bringing about the end of serfdom, higher wages and improved peasant prosperity, the introduction of more women into the labour force and the emergence of the nuclear family as the main economic unit. There are, of course – as with each model on offer to us – historians who challenge the validity of part or all of this narrative. But we seek here only to establish the general shape of the model for the purposes of asking whether Wales followed this demographically driven cycle of economic expansion, crisis and contraction, and to what extent it shared in the socioeconomic transformation that occurred in England following the depopulation of the Black Death.[8]

The narrative of observable expansion and contraction in the Welsh economy, as set out in the first three chapters of this book, lends itself broadly to the demographic model, albeit on a slightly different timeline from that of England. It is worth revisiting this point in some detail, because demographic change in Wales is relevant to all models of economic change, not just the 'demographic model' which takes population as the economic prime mover. With respect to the basic premise that population will grow so long as surplus resources are available, this holds true for medieval Wales, insofar as Welsh population probably grew steadily, if not dramatically, until the early twelfth century (Chapter 1, Demographic change to *c*.1100). Place names attest to this. The earliest surviving land surveys from the thirteenth century often indicate that the *hendref*, or 'old settlement', lands belonging to a *gwely* contained the best lowland arable – often strips in open fields – while simultaneously being the most intensely subdivided through partible gavelkind inheritance among all male children of the *gwely*.[9]
The *gwely* system was dependent on regular territorial expansion. In the absence of additional arable lands for assart or annexation, expansion was achieved by intergenerational partitioning of arable and the addition of a 'girdle' of upland pasture surrounding the original *hendref* arable. Where bond communities existed, they tended to be concentrated on productive arable, hemmed in by semi-free and free *gwelyau* on more marginal soils.[10] As Glanville Jones has argued, gavelkind inheritance as practised by *gwelyau* in native Wales appears initially 'to have encouraged a high rate of population growth' but also to have 'contained within itself the seeds of a fairly rapid decline', as 'the continued operation of gavelkind reduced the arable stakes of some heirs below the economic minimum'.[11] It is difficult to pinpoint when this state was reached. Jones suggests that the last new 'clanlands' of the *gwelyau* emerged in the twelfth century.[12]

It would seem that, unlike England, Wales did not experience sustained or extensive population growth across the period 1067–1300. The internal colonisation of marginal lands across Wales, whether voluntarily through the proliferation of semi-free and free *gwelyau* in areas of native control or of necessity where Anglo-Norman colonisers expelled native agriculturalists from lowland to upland areas, probably served to increase the net productivity of Wales and support a degree of population growth (see Chapter 1, The impact of rural colonisation). But, as a resource-constrained area, in which no more than 14 per cent of the land is croppable, scope for demographic and economic growth was limited at an early stage.[13] It is likely that as early as 1100 only 'marginal' lands remained to be newly exploited (see above, Chapter 1, Demographic change to *c*.1100). Certainly, the best proxy measure of demographic growth available, at least for areas under native control, is the settlement of these 'marginal' lands after 1100, suggesting by 1300 a non-urban population increase of at least 35 per cent but certainly no more than 70 per cent.[14] Thus, the Anglo-Norman conquest expropriated lands from people living in a landscape already 'at capacity' and was probably itself the cause of serious short-term depopulation and economic dislocation in conjunction with English immigration. The long-term consequences of colonisation included economic growth associated with low-level urbanisation, commutation, increased trade and other advancements, and it established an immigrant elite that perpetuated its economic superiority by dominating corn production and exchange. But there is no direct evidence of colonial increases in agricultural productivity sufficient to fuel post-colonisation rural population growth. Only the establishment of towns, particularly larger towns comprising primarily English immigrant communities, provides evidence of colonisation contributing directly to population growth, of no more than 25 per cent, indicated by the 20 per cent share of the population of Wales living in towns by 1300 (see Chapter 1, Commutation and urbanisation; Chapter 2, Urbanisation and immigration).[15] Overall, a realistic estimate of population increase in Wales, 1067 to 1300, would be perhaps 70 to 80 per cent, made up of a middling estimate rural growth as represented by movement onto marginal lands along with the new urban population. This is hardly comparable to the increase of as much as 200 per cent, or trebling, of the English population within this same time frame, and *was not* the result of a rapid opening up of abundant and previously underutilized resources.[16]

The 'demographic' model, as applied in an English setting, 1066 to 1300, suggests that population growth fuelled increased agricultural production, often on newly opened-up lands, which in turn led to economic growth, expressed as rising seigniorial incomes rooted in profitable demesne agriculture and rising rents, blossoming urbanisation and an intensification of trade. This model does not fit Wales, where population growth was less than half of that experienced in England; rising seigniorial incomes were more likely to have been the product of an intensification of arbitrary taxation; almost all urbanisation was an external imposition underpinned by immigration; and trade networks were by-products of the interlinked forces of top-down commutation, bottom-up exchange to meet tax demands and urban market networks extending back to England. The economy of Wales certainly grew dramatically as a result of these developments, but such change was neither primarily demographically driven nor – with the exception of some later moves toward commutation by Welsh princes – internally generated.[17]

In Wales, famine in 1315–22 and plague from 1348–9 together probably led to the death of more than one-third of the population – a bare minimum for plague mortality alone in England – and caused severe economic disruption (see above, Chapter 3, Crisis and restructuring).[18] But there are few grounds on which to view these events as Malthusian 'positive checks'. If, in a narrow sense, a 'positive check' occurs as a result of population increasing exponentially while food production increases only arithmetically, then the English experience of the Great Famine of 1315–22 can be attributed to the intersection between England's as much as trebling of population between 1066 and 1300, and the – at best – doubling of food production over the same period, exacerbated by the three years of appalling weather after 1315.[19] The Black Death, it has been suggested by Slavin, could then have wrought a linked wave of destruction upon an immune-deficient generation of famine survivors.[20] But in Wales, where agricultural resources were already scarce by 1100 and population increase from 1067 to 1300 was a more modest 70 to 80 per cent with a compound growth rate of just 0.25 per cent per annum (PCPA), population growth much more closely approximated increases in food production.[21] That is to say, while the Great Famine was arguably a 'check' on the population in Wales, it was the result of a population long vulnerable on the margins of subsistence suffering misfortunes prompted by the exogenous force of harvest-depressing bad weather and cattle-decimating murrain. It was not, as some have claimed for England, a Malthusian 'positive check', the exceptional intensity of which resulted, at least in part, from the endogenous force of rapidly growing population – of perhaps 0.47 PCPA, 1086–1300, and even 0.78 PCPA, 1200–1300 – colliding abruptly with the limits of food production.[22] Also, Slavin's claim that the deprivations of famine may have created an immune-deficient generation especially susceptible to the plague three decades later supposes that cattle murrain led to protein deficiencies in children's diets arising from dairy shortages. Such deficiencies are unlikely to have been as acute in Wales as they were in the arable expanses of champion England, despite murrain, because of Wales's relatively large upland cattle sector and typically more protein-rich diet.[23]

But what of the effects of depopulation from the mid-fourteenth century? Did a decline in population create a 'Golden Age of Labour' as it is held to have done in England? As argued above, this probably did not occur (see Chapter 3, Challenges to the Englishries). The cost of labour after the plague in Wales increased to about 150 per cent of pre-plague levels, an increase sufficient to motivate lords to try to regulate workers' wages, but opportunities for paid labour would have been limited by the relatively small proportion of Wales under the plough which, as we have seen, was probably less than 14 per cent of the land area, and the less labour-intensive nature pastoral agriculture. Food prices, especially for grains, did not drop in Wales from the 1370s to as great an extent as they did in England, instead remaining closer to mid-fourteenth-century highs. What gains were made by Welsh peasants and labourers in this period were almost certainly wiped out in marcher lordships by the intensification of judicial lordship and arbitrary taxation. Nor, for native Welsh women at least, did post-plague depopulation open up new opportunities for work and greater social independence, as has been argued for England.[24] Instead, the right of Welsh women to possess property established in the Principality by the 1284 Statute of Wales, and progressively extended to native women in the lordships across the fourteenth and fifteenth centuries, was of more profound significance.

Did depopulation lead to the decline of serfdom and the emergence of the nuclear-family farmstead, as has been suggested for England?[25] Certainly in Wales, the *gwely*, as the heart of communal agricultural and legal responsibility, declined after the Black Death, and serfdom disappeared (see Chapter 3, The collapse of the *gwely*). However, serfdom had always been of limited significance in conquest-era Wales, focused on the old princely demesnes of the north-west and the most intensively colonised Englishries of the south-east, and light by English standards in other areas. Here, depopulation may have effectively liberated the serfs, whose bargaining power was improved by a low labour-to-land ratio, and who either renegotiated their tenue or fled to another estate where free tenure could be attained. The decline of the *gwely*, however, had its first seeds in the process of conquest and escheat, and in the fabric of the Statute of Wales, which undermined both the territorial integrity and the legal-economic significance of the *gwely*. The Black Death no doubt resulted in further decline, and depopulation rendered some *gwelyau* unworkable, with too few hands to manage the land and contribute to financial obligations. Nevertheless, it was the wave of confiscations following the Glyndŵr rebellion and rise of the land-hungry squirearchy that would provide the *coup de grâce* (see, Chapter 3, After Glyndŵr). As the *gwely* passed, so the independent smallholder and local squire came to replace it.

Neo-Marxism and class struggle

The Middle Ages have proved to be a fertile ground for an array of Marxist-influenced scholars who have sought to understand medieval social and economic change through the lens of class relations and class struggle.[26] For those historians who have adopted this perspective, the relationship between the owners of the means of production, such as landlords or employers, and those who provide productive labour, such as peasants or wage-labourers, is necessarily conflictual, with such relations and conflicts being a key determinant of the form and direction of social and economic development, with change in this economic 'base' in turn affecting the whole legal, social and cultural 'superstructure' of society.[27] Particularly influential has been the work of Rodney Hilton, whose classic 1973 study of medieval peasant movements continues to be a starting point for investigations of what has been called the 'crisis of feudalism'.[28] This was an international medieval 'crisis', first identified by the (non-Marxist) French historian, Marc Bloch, in his 1931 volume *French Rural History*, which was characterised by falling seigniorial incomes, a loss of lordly control over unfree tenants and an end to profitable demesne agriculture.[29] For those historians who focus on the rise and fall of population as an explanation of economic change, this crisis was the result of overpopulation and declining peasant prosperity by the early 1300s and was then intensified through the shock of Black Death, high mortality and the subsequent flight of unfree tenants and the collapse of seigniorial income. By contrast, for Hilton, and other Marxists such as Robert Brenner, 'the central feature was a crisis of relationships between the two main classes of feudal society, which had begun before the demographic collapse and continued, even in some altered forms, during and after it.'[30] For Hilton, as for Guy Bois in his 1976 monograph on Normandy, it was the relations between peasants and landlords, not demographic 'Malthusian' factors, which constituted the prime determinant of economic development.[31]

Thus, in England, from the late twelfth to the mid-fourteenth century, landlords are perceived to have tightened the screws of social control through the elaboration of the inferior legal position of many peasants, in particular by excluding the unfree from access to the developing common law and intensifying surplus extraction through ever-increasing land rents and manorial fines that unfree tenants, lacking access to common law, are held to be powerless to resist. In turn, such restrictions and impositions are seen as hindering economic development and so being the cause of the Malthusian crisis of overpopulation of the early fourteenth century. The demographic downturn of the fourteenth century is seen as intensifying class conflict, although with divergent outcomes in different areas of Europe. In England, the peasants gained the upper hand through collective resistance, securing lower rents and greater personal freedoms in which resided the origins of 'agrarian capitalism'.[32] This fundamental disagreement between 'Marxist' and 'Malthusian' medieval historians became explicit in the 'Brenner Debate' following the 1976 publication of an influential article by Brenner on 'Agrarian Class Structure and Economic Development in Pre-industrial Europe'.[33] The central thesis of this article was that a Marxist interpretation of the 'crisis of feudalism', emphasizing the success of western European peasants in loosing feudal bonds, explains the emergence of the 'agrarian capitalist' and eventually capitalism in the west, particularly in England, while at the same time the failure of peasants in eastern Europe in their struggle against the landowning elite resulted in the further development of serfdom in the east.[34] That is to say, given similar population trends, the outcome of class struggle could dictate divergent trajectories of economic change. This discussion was amplified, challenged and elaborated in a series of related articles in the respected journal *Past and Present*.[35]

Although the 'Brenner debate' provoked discussion of a number of different regions across Europe, Wales was nowhere mentioned in the edited volume of articles reprinting the core of *The Brenner Debate*.[36] Similarly, although the most recent defence of Brenner's arguments has been mounted by an historian who has researched medieval Welsh history, it presents the creation of towns in Wales, in step with English conquest, as simply an expression of lords' novel strategies to enhance their pre-plague incomes, and argues that in post-plague 'southern Wales . . . agrarian capitalism developed simultaneously to England in the shell of English lordly estates'.[37] In other words, as infamously printed in the 1888 *Encyclopaedia Britannica*, 'Wales, *see* England'.

Yet, perhaps the absence of Wales from this discussion should come as no surprise. After all, at the very core of the Marxist 'crisis of feudalism' is a clash between exploited unfree tenants and the landowning class, whereas in late medieval Wales the unfree were relatively few in number, being located principally, as we have seen, in the heavily colonised south-east and princely demesnes of the north-west, and had comparatively light obligations by English standards.[38] Indeed, even for England, one of the main criticisms that has been levelled at Marxist interpretations of the 'crisis' of feudalism is that even in relatively unfree late thirteenth-century eastern and midland England less than half of households were unfree and they held only around 30 per cent of all land.[39] Thus, quite apart from the general reluctance of scholars of England to grapple with the complex patchwork of seigniorial governance in Wales, it would seem that there is little incentive for Marxists to engage critically with the history of a confusingly multi-ethnic place where the prevalence of peasant freedom offers little scope for discussion of the struggle of bond men and women to be free.

Nevertheless, the Marxist stress on the role of class struggle in generating social and economic change does have the potential to illuminate the history of medieval Wales. But to realise this potential, historians would have to cease focusing narrowly on the relationship between lords and serfs. Instead, one might consider the English lords as one class, and the Welsh peasants, who were most acutely to feel the caprices of escheat, judicial lordship and arbitrary taxation in the fourteenth and fifteenth centuries, as another (see Chapter 2, Lordship and society; Chapter 3, Challenges to the Englishries). Was then, the forced retention of partible inheritance, which gave rise to 'fat profits' from fines to alienate land, an act of top-down class conflict?[40] From this perspective, was the post-plague attempt of English lords to exploit traditional Welsh dues, such as *amobr*, in an attempt to offset falling revenues, and the complaints of the native community about that, a form of class warfare? Likewise, could we adopt a similar perspective on the royal prohibition against Welshmen becoming burgesses in new towns versus the large number of Welsh who nevertheless did so in the early fourteenth century, in some instances only to be dispossessed a few decades later? Could the Glyndŵr rebellion of 1400–16 then be viewed as a Welsh equivalent to the English Peasants' Revolt of 1381?

Any characterisation of these events as class struggle raises theoretical and empirical problems. What ought we to make of the English peasant colonisers, especially the bondmen of Gwent, who had perhaps the heaviest labour services in Wales?[41] Likewise, how should we view the dozen or more towns predominantly populated by Welsh burgesses from their inception to 1536 and beyond, such as Newborough (Anglesey)?[42] Just as a peasant cultivator might be Welsh or English, so too might a labourer, artisan or merchant. Perhaps then, ethnic groups ought better to be considered 'systacts' sharing a common location in one or more of the three dimensions of social structure identified by Walter Runciman, the economic, the ideological (i.e. status/prestige) and the coercive (i.e. power to induce others to do things, whether they wish to or not), rather than simply as economic classes?[43] Faced with these conundrums, ethnicity ceases to be a suitable proxy for class, and the Marxist model ceases to be applicable. If one privileges ethnicity over class as a tool for analysis then this is to adopt a Weberian emphasis on status and on the effects of political conquest rather than to employ a Marxist focus on society's economic 'base' and on class relations arising out of the production process. It moves the analysis in a very different direction, viewing persons as members of multiple overlapping, and often competing, self-interest groups. This is the 'social closure' model, yet another, if less widely adopted, model for understanding late medieval society – employed most notably in an English context by Stephen Rigby – that has not yet been tested against Wales.[44]

The commercialisation model

The commercialisation model is by far the simplest approach to outline. It has its roots in the work of late nineteenth- and early twentieth-century pre-modern historians who first investigated the economy of Britain employing the 'supply and demand' economics developed by Adam Smith in the late eighteenth century. The main themes of this work which are relevant for our purposes are its stress on the long-term growth of the market and on the consequent growing division of labour within society as leading to increases in economic efficiency and productivity.⁴⁵ For these authors, the emergence and proliferation of trade and markets, and the increasing circulation of coinage, were key to understanding an almost monolithic and irresistible 'rise' of towns, manufactures and the middle class, penetrating manorial economics as an external force and liberating peasants from serfdom through market forces. Edward Lewis exemplified this school of thought when publishing his pioneer works on 'The Development of Industry and Commerce in Wales', *The Medieval Boroughs of Snowdonia* and 'A Contribution to the Commercial History of Wales' (see Introduction).⁴⁶ In his words, 'market and fair organizations . . . gradually revolutionised the primitive conditions of the Welsh economy . . . [and] . . . the conditions of the new economy were more conducive to social and commercial development.'⁴⁷

This body of literature was challenged in the middle part of the twentieth century by the demographic model, and its emphasis on the role of demographic change as the prime mover of economic expansion and contraction, and by the neo-Marxist model and its emphasis on the capacity of social relations to accelerate, decelerate or even reverse economic trends (as above). But since the 1990s, influenced in part by the perceived inadequacies of the demographic and neo-Marxist models, and capitalising on the ever-increasing volume of data generated by economic historians, a 'new' commercialisation model has arisen. Perhaps best set out in the work of Richard Britnell, this renewed interest in commercialisation has focused on a number of measurable aspects of medieval life, prominent among which are urbanisation, monetisation and economic specialisation, while remaining sensitive to the reality that these factors may be of increasing or decreasing importance at any given place or time, dependent on a number of variables, such as demographic change or landlord-peasant relations.⁴⁸ The current generation of scholars of commercialisation emphasise the interconnectedness of these factors as, for instance, when those peasants not able to maintain themselves in an increasingly crowded countryside before 1348–9 moved into towns, where urban population density in turn encouraged specialisation within both town and surrounding countryside, which in turn increased efficiency. By the time of the Black Death, social attitudes towards money, the use of the market and towns had changed sufficiently for these institutions to continue to thrive after depopulation.[49] Most recently, efforts have been made to produce a 'theoretical formulation' elaborating the 'powerful conjunction between entrepreneurial activity and population growth ... [noting that] ... the former tended to lead to the latter', while emphasizing that 'in normal circumstances, it was individuals and families who called the shots, and it was certainly they who fashioned both commercial activity and population growth.'[50]

The commercialisation model fits well with some aspects of the economic history of Wales, particularly its urban history. The introduction of towns into Wales by Norman and English invaders, followed by the 'flood of silver' from England in the thirteenth century, rapidly monetised and urbanised Welsh society (see, Chapter 1, Commutation and urbanisation; Chapter 2, Urbanisation and immigration). While the foreign imposition of this change, concomitant with only modest pre-plague domestic population growth, augmented by English immigration, suggests the limited extent to which commercialisation may have stimulated population increase, what is particularly impressive is the durability of this fundamental change.[51] Both urbanism and English-style manors relying heavily on unfree labour were introduced into Wales by conquerors from only the late eleventh century. Yet urban life would endure the rigours of both the Black Death and the Glyndŵr rebellion while, following the Black Death, the manorial system in Wales succumbed 'in a year or two' (see, Chapter 3, Challenges to the Englishries).[52]

Specialisation is not always easy to see in Wales, particularly in the countryside. It is perhaps most visible in the emergence of the cloth industry, and construction of numerous fulling mills in Wales, both before and after the period of Glyndŵr's revolt (see Chapter 3, After Glyndŵr). It could also be argued that the cattle industry specialised in this period, particularly in primarily upland lordships such as Brecon (see Chapter 2, Lordship and society). Specialization is generally more visible in urban settings, where it could prove durable. For example at Ruthin (Denbighshire), skinners, tanners, glovers and cobblers all contributed to a leather goods industry already comprising the town's largest concentration of skilled craftsmen in the 1320s, later reflected in the establishment of a 'Brotherhood of Corvisers and Shoemakers' in 1496.[53] But the development of the Welsh economy and of market-orientated specialisation was hindered by two factors. The first was the destruction brought about by the Glyndŵr rebellion, especially the burning of at least forty towns and subsequent failure of many, followed closely by the pan-European depression of the fifteenth century. The second was the post-Glyndŵr drain of fiscal, and especially human capital to England, as a net outflow of immigration headed east of Offa's Dyke in search of unskilled work, apprenticeship and a better life.

There are of course other models which might be employed in explaining the economy of medieval Wales. Weberian social closure, focusing on overlapping and competing groups within society, and now associated with the work of Rigby, has already been mentioned.[54] More recently, Bruce Campbell has set out in detail the case for considering the environment to be a central factor in shaping long-term trends in economic change.[55] However, perhaps the real 'elephant in the room' in any discussion of late medieval Wales is of course the role of English conquest. How might native social institutions have developed if not for political competition with, and conquest by, Wales's closest neighbour (see, Chapter 1, The organisation of native society)? When would Wales have monetised and urbanised without the imposition through conquest of a money economy and urban life? Would the Welsh economy then not have become so dependent on the English? Similarly, without the English conquest, Glyndŵr's rebellion would never have occurred or stifled the fifteenth-century economy. These are important, potentially constructive questions, but this kind of counterfactual history of 'what if' can quickly descend into mere speculation. Whether choosing to privilege one model of economic development over another, or estimating what questions of counterfactual history are or are not constructive, the historian is ultimately choosing to ascribe historical primacy, whether universal or specific, to one factor over another, and this 'will depend not upon historical reality but upon our particular context and purposes'.⁵⁶ In practice, most historians tend towards 'a theoretical eclecticism and to marry the strengths of each of the different approaches on offer'.⁵⁷ The first three chapters of this book represent an attempt to do just that.

A better approach to assessing economic change in Wales than working through the lens of one or more of the above models as a starting point is instead to keep in mind a number of factors one must take into consideration for the purpose of analysing the medieval economy in the context of Wales, while using the above or other models of economic change as tools of investigation. The three factors set out here run through and beyond the so-called 'Age of Conquest'. They reflect the most prominent recurrent themes of this volume.

The first factor is conquest. Conquest altered the trajectory of almost every native social and economic institution, down to the very building block of the *gwely*. It directly or indirectly introduced fundamental and permanent changes, such as urbanisation and monetisation. It altered the ethnic composition of Wales and created innumerable familial and economic linkages with the land of the conqueror. It would give rise to the preponderance of documentary sources through which the historian views social and economic organisation and production in medieval Wales.

The second factor is ethnic difference. Ethnic difference explains the nature of post-conquest settlement. It led to the ghettoisation of Welsh tenants in de facto or legally defined Welshries. It was the premise on which the regalian power of marcher lords was based. It led to the differential treatment of English and Welsh tenants, excusing the more immoderate economic exploitation of the latter through arbitrary taxation and ethnic-specific fines such as *amobr*. Welsh tenure, retained by English lords, retarded the growth of the native land market and the intergenerational concentration of heritable wealth. In times of economic hardship ethnicity was the basis of the exclusion of Welsh persons from the mercantile class, as from some post-plague towns. It facilitated the sense of shared grievance that underpinned the Glyndŵr rebellion and the endemic disorder that followed it, crippling the fifteenth-century economy.

The third factor is geography. Geography explains the poor calorie producing potential and modest demographic growth of Wales. It contributed to the political disunity that expedited conquest and concomitant economic transformation. Wales's distinctive mountainous stretches led to the characterisation of 'Welsh' as 'upland', and helped Norman and English administrators to rationalise the ghettoisation of the Welsh in upland areas. Geography dictated England as Wales's main trading partner after commercialisation.

These three factors, more than any others, serve collectively to explain the changing shape of the economy of Wales from William fitz Osbern's initial 1067 foray into Gwent, to Henry VIII's Act of Union of 1536. They are also factors with a unique relevance to Wales, highlighting the need to investigate the economic history of Wales in its own right, rather than viewing it as a thread woven into the narrative of English economic history. Equally, the classic supermodels of economic change have only limited application for Wales. Wales itself may yet provide the best comparator for future analyses of other small nations of medieval Europe.

Notes

1 J. Hatcher and M. Bailey, *Modelling the Middle Ages: The History and Theory of England's Economic Development* (Oxford, 2001), pp. 11–20.
2 Hatcher and Bailey, *Modelling the Middle Ages*.
3 A. D. Carr, *Medieval Anglesey*, 2nd edn (Llangefni, 2011), p. 126.
4 T. R. Malthus, *An Essay on the Principle of Population* (London 1798); for a modern introduction see S. H. Rigby, *English Society in the Later Middle Ages: Class, Status and Gender* (Houndmills, 1995), pp. 66–9; D. B. Grigg, *Population Growth and Agrarian Change: An Historical Prospective* (Cambridge, 1980).
5 Hatcher and Bailey, *Modelling the Middle Ages*, p. 29.

6   See, W. C. Jordan, *The Great Famine: Northern Europe in the Early Fourteenth Century* (Princeton, 1996); For the English famine see I. Kershaw, 'The Great Famine and Agrarian Crisis in England, 1315–1322', *P&P*, 59 (1973), 3–50.
7   Hatcher and Bailey, *Modelling the Middle Ages*, pp. 28–33. For nutritional deficiencies, namely protein shortage, see, P. Slavin, 'The Great Bovine Pestilence and its Eonomic and Evironmental Consequences in England and Wales', *EcHR*, 65 (2012), 1255–60.
8   For a concise rendering of key objections see S. H. Rigby, 'Introduction: social structure and economic change in late medieval England', in R. Horrox and W. M. Ormrod (eds), *A Social History of England, 1200–1500* (Cambridge, 2006), pp. 17–20.
9   G. R. J. Jones, 'The Tribal System in Wales: A Re-assessment in Light of Settlement Studies', *WHR*, 1 (1960–3), 117.
10 G. R. J. Jones, 'The Distribution of Medieval Settlement in Anglesey', *TransAng*. (1955), 287.
11 Jones, 'The Tribal System', 117.
12 G. R. J. Jones, 'Post-Roman Wales' in H. P. R. Finberg (ed.), *AgHist.*, vol. I, part II: *A.D. 43–1042* (Cambridge, 1972), p. 331.
13 Armstrong, 'Research Briefing: The Farming Sector in Wales', *National Assembly for Wales Research Service*, paper 16–053 (2016), 6.
14 Jones, 'The Distribution of Medieval Settlement', 36, 50–3.
15 Soulsby, *Towns*, pp. 16, 19–24.
16 Hatcher and Bailey, *Modelling the Middle Ages*, p. 29; English population was most recently re-estimated by Broadberry et al. as growing from 1.71 million in 1086 to 4.81 million in 1348. S. Broadberry, B. M. S. Campbell, A. Klein, M. Overton and B. van Leeuwen, *British Economic Growth, 1270–1870* (Cambridge, 2015), pp. 20–2, 72–3, 114–20 (figures 1.06, 3.04 and tables 3.16–3.19).
17 T. Jones Pierce, 'The growth of commutation in Gwynedd in the thirteenth century', in *WelshSoc.*, pp. 103–26.
18 C. Platt, *King Death: The Black Death and its Aftermath in Late-Medieval England* (London, 1996), pp. 1–18.
19 Doubling of food production reflects a doubling of land under cultivation, with increases in productivity on good soils offset by the increased cultivation of less productive 'marginal' soils. Hatcher and Bailey, *Modelling the Middle Ages*, p. 29; Broadberry et al., *British*

Economic Growth, pp. 72–3, 114–20 (figure 3.04 and tables 3.16–3.19); For a summary of the English narrative see Rigby, 'Introduction', pp. 25–7; For an alternative, climate-focused view on the causes of famine see B. Campbell, *The Great Transition: Climate, Disease and Society in the Late-Medieval World* (Cambridge, 2016), pp. 332–48.

20 Slavin, 'The Great Bovine Pestilence', 1255–60; Marxist historians have also emphasised the possibility of this famine-plague linkage. See for commentary Hatcher and Bailey, *Modelling the Middle Ages*, p. 110; Brenner, 'The Agrarian Roots of European Capitalism', 63, n.104.

21 If the population of Wales was 250,000 to 300,000 persons c.1300, as a result of an 80% increase in the population of c.1067, then the initial population would have been between 139,000 and 167,000 persons.

22 Hatcher and Bailey, *Modelling the Middle Ages*, pp. 27–8, 52–5 (citing Michael Postan and others); J. Langdon and J. Masschaele, 'Commercial Activity and Population Growth in Medieval England', *P&P*, 190 (2006), 64–8.

23 Stevens, 'The Great Famine', 25–30; Schofield, 'Wales and the Great Famine', 152.

24 P. J. P. Goldberg, *Women, Work, and Life Cycle in a Medieval Economy: Women in York and Yorkshire, c.1300–1520* (Oxford, 1992); J. M. Bennett, 'England: women and gender', in S. H. Rigby (ed.), *A Companion to Britain in the Later Middle Ages* (Oxford, 2003), pp. 87–106.

25 Platt, *King Death*, pp. 33–47.

26 For a survey, see S. H. Rigby, 'Historical Materialism: Social Structure and Social Change in the Middle Ages', *Journal of Medieval and Early Modern Studies*, 34 (2004), 473–522.

27 Elegantly set out by Hatcher and Bailey, *Modelling the Middle Ages*, p. 69.

28 R. H. Hilton, *Bond Men Made Free: Medieval Peasant Movements and the English Rising of 1381* (London, 1973).

29 For a modern overview, see D. McNally, *Political Economy and the Rise of Capitalism: A Reinterpretation* (Berkeley, 1988), pp. 2–15, cit. 2.; M. Bloch, *French Rural History: An Essay on its Basic Characteristics* (1931), trans. J. Sondheimer (London, 1966), chapter 3, pp. 64–101.

30 R. H. Hilton, 'A Crisis of Feudalism', *P&P*, 80 (1978), 3–19.

31 G. Bois, *The Crisis of Feudalism: Economy and Society in Eastern Normandy, c. 1300–1550* (Cambridge, 1976).
32 'Agrarian capitalism' is best associated, in English historiography, with, R. Brenner, 'Agrarian Class Structure and Economic Development in Pre-industrial Europe', *P&P*, 70 (1976), 30–75; R. Brenner, 'The Agrarian Roots of European Capitalism', *P&P*, 97 (1982), 16–113.
33 Brenner, 'Agrarian Class Structure'.
34 For a summary, see S. H. Rigby, *English Society in the Later Middle Ages: Class, Status and Gender* (Houndmills, 1995), pp. 127–33.
35 T. H. Aston and C. H. E. Philpin (eds), *The Brenner Debate: Agrarian Class Structure and Economic Development in Pre-industrial Europe* (Cambridge, 1985).
36 Hilton, *Bond Men Made Free*.
37 S. Dimmock, *The Origin of Capitalism in England, 1400–1600* (Leiden, 2014), pp. 164, 200–1.
38 T. Jones Pierce, 'Medieval Cardiganshire – a study in social origins', in *WelshSoc.*, pp. 309–27.
39 Hatcher and Bailey, *Modelling the Middle Ages*, p. 99.
40 Ll. B. Smith, 'The Gage and the Land Market in Medieval Wales', *EcHR*, 29 (1976), 539–41
41 *SouthWales*, pp. 157–73.
42 M. F. Stevens, 'Anglo-Welsh towns of the early fourteenth century: a survey of urban origins, property-holding and ethnicity', in *UrbanCult.*, p. 140.
43 W. G. Runciman, *A Treatise on Social Theory, vol. 2: Substantive Social Theory* (Cambridge, 1989), pp. 12–17, 20–7. Assessing Runciman and others, see R. Kreckel, 'Dimensions of Social Inequality – Conceptual Analysis and Theory of Society', *Sociologische Gids*, 23 (1976), 338–62.
44 S. H. Rigby, *English Society*.
45 Rigby, 'Introduction', pp. 10–12; Rigby, *English Society*, pp, 61–5.
46 E. A. Lewis, 'The Development of Industry and Commerce in Wales during the Middle Ages', *TransRoyal*, new series, 17 (1903), 121–73; *The Medieval Boroughs of Snowdonia* (London, 1912); 'A Contribution to the Commercial History of Medieval Wales', *Y Cymmrodor*, 24 (1913), 86–188.
47 Lewis, 'A Contribution', 88–9.

48 R. H. Britnell, "Commercialisation and economic development in England, 1000–1300', in R. H. Britnell and B. M. S. Campbell (eds), *A Commercialising Economy: England, 1086 to c.1300* (Manchester, 1995), pp. 7–26; R. H. Britnell, *The Commercialisation of English Society, 1000–1500* (Cambridge, 1993).
49 Britnell, *The Commercialisation*, pp. 228–37.
50 Langdon and Masschaele, 'Commercial Activity', 36, 81.
51 Langdon and Masschaele, 'Commercial Activity', 35–81.
52 P. Ziegler, *The Black Death*, 2nd edn (London, 1998), p. 201 (quotation); W. Rees, 'The Black Death in Wales', *TransRoyal*, 4th series, 3 (1920), 115–35.
53 M. F. Stevens, *Urban Assimilation in Post-Conquest Wales: Ethnicity, Gender and Economy in Ruthin, 1282–1348* (Cardiff, 2010), pp. 232, 235–9, 248.
54 Rigby, *English Society*, pp. 9–14, 303–23.
55 Campbell, *The Great Transition*.
56 S. H. Rigby, 'Historical Causation: Is One Thing More Important than Another?', *History*, 80 (1995), 242.
57 Rigby, 'Introduction', p. 30.

BIBLIOGRAPHY

Primary sources

Manuscripts

The National Archives, PRO SC 2/215/45 to SC 2/221/11 – Dyffryn Clwyd Court Rolls.

National Library of Wales, SA/MISC/196 – Inquisition concerning the township of Vaynol.

Royal Commission on the Ancient and Historical Monuments of Wales, NPRN 24219.

Published

Bowen, I. (ed.), *The Statutes of Wales* (London, 1908).

Davies, R. R., and Ll. Smith (eds), machine readable database, *The Dyffryn Clwyd Court Roll Database, 1294–1422* (Aberystwyth, 1995); ESRC awards R000232548 and R000234070, available from the UK Data Archive, *http://www.data-archive.ac.uk/*.

Ellis, H. (ed.), *Registrum Vulgariter Nuncupatum: The Record of Caernarvon* (London, 1838).

Haydon, F. S. (ed.), *Eulogium Historiarum sive Temporis: Chronicon ab Orbe Condito Usque ad Annum Domini M.CCC.LXVI, a Monacho Quodam Malmesburiensi Exaratum* (London, 1863).

Jack, R. I., 'Records of Denbighshire Lordships, II: The Lordship of Dyffryn Clwyd in 1324', *DHST*, 17 (1968), 7–53.

Thorpe, L. (trans.), *Gerald of Wales: The Journey through Wales and The Description of Wales* (London, 1978).

Williams-Jones, K. (ed.), *The Merioneth Lay Subsidy Roll, 1292–3* (Cardiff, 1976).

Secondary sources

Allen, M., *Mints and Money in Medieval England* (Cambridge, 2012).

Altschul, M., 'The lordship of Glamorgan and Morgannwg, 1217–1317, I: Glamorgan and Morgannwg under the rule of the De Clare family', in *GlamCH*, pp. 45–72.

Armstrong, E., 'Research Briefing: The Farming Sector in Wales', *National Assembly for Wales Research Service*, paper 16–053 (2016).

Aston, T. H., and C. H. E. Philpin (eds), *The Brenner Debate: Agrarian Class Structure and Economic Development in Pre-industrial Europe* (Cambridge, 1985).

Bailey, M., *A Marginal Economy? East Anglian Breckland in the Later Middle Ages* (Cambridge, 1989).

Bailey, M., 'The myth of the "seigniorial reaction" in England after the Black Death', in M. Kowaleski, J. Langdon and P. R. Schofield (eds), *Peasants and Lords in the Medieval English Economy: Essays in Honour of Bruce M. S. Campbell* (Turnhout, 2015), pp. 147–72.

Barrell, A. D. M., and M. H. Brown, 'A Settler Community in Post-conquest Rural Wales', *WHR*, 17 (1995), 332–55.

Barrell, A. D. M., and R. R. Davies, 'Land, Lineage, and Revolt in North-east Wales, 1243–1441: A Case Study', *Cambrian Medieval Celtic Studies*, 29 (1995), 27–51.

Barton, P. G., 'Gruffudd ap Gwenwynwyn's Trefnant market charter, 1279–1282', *Montgomeryshire Collections*, 90 (2002), 69–86.

Bateson, M., 'The Laws of Breteuil', *The English Historical Review*, 15 and 16 (1900–1), [vol. 15] 73–8, 302–18, 496–523, 754–7; [vol. 16] 92–110, 332–45.

Beresford, M., *New Towns of the Middle Ages: Town Plantation in England, Wales and Gascony* (New York, 1967).

Bloch, M., *French Rural History: An Essay on Its Basic Characteristics* (1931), trans. J. Sondheimer (London, 1966).

Blockmans, W., and P. Hoppenbrouwers, *Introduction to Medieval Europe, 300–1500*, 2nd edn (London, 2014).

Bois, G., *The Crisis of Feudalism: Economy and Society in Eastern Normandy, c. 1300–1550* (Cambridge, 1976).

Bolton, J., *The Medieval English Economy, 1150–1500* (London, 1980).

Bolton, J., *Money in the Medieval English Economy, 973–1498* (Manchester, 2012).

Brenner, R., 'Agrarian Class Structure and Economic Development in Pre-industrial Europe', *P&P*, 70 (1976), 30–75.

Brenner, R., 'The Agrarian Roots of European Capitalism', *P&P*, 97 (1982), 16–113.

Britnell, R. H., 'Commercialisation and economic development in England, 1000–1300', in R. H. Britnell and B. M. S. Campbell (eds), *A Commercialising Economy: England, 1086 to c.1300* (Manchester, 1995), pp. 7–26.

Britnell, R. H., *The Commercialisation of English Society, 1000–1500*, 2nd edn (Cambridge, 1996).

Britnell, R., *Britain and Ireland, 1050–1530* (Oxford, 2004).

Broadberry, S., B. M. S. Campbell, A. Klein, M. Overton and B. van Leeuwen, *British Economic Growth, 1270–1870* (Cambridge, 2015).

Burtscher, M., *The Fitzalans: Earls of Arundel and Surrey, Lords of the Welsh Marches, 1267–1415* (Little Logaston, 2008).

Butler, L. A. S., 'Wales', in H. E. Hallman (ed.), *AgHist.*, vol. II: 1042–1350 (Cambridge, 1988), pp. 933–65.

Butler, L.A.S., 'Rural building in England and Wales: Wales', in
E. Miller (ed.), *AgHist.*, vol. III: 1348–1500 (Cambridge, 1991),
pp. 894–919.
Campbell, B., 'Arable Productivity in Medieval England: Some
Evidence from Norfolk', *EcHR*, 43 (1983), 397–404.
Campbell, B., *English Seigniorial Agriculture, 1250–1450* (Cambridge,
2000).
Campbell, B., 'Benchmarking Medieval Economic Development:
England, Wales, Scotland and Ireland, c.1290', *EcHR*, 61 (2008),
896–948.
Campbell, B., *The Great Transition: Climate, Disease and Society in the
Late-Medieval World* (Cambridge, 2016).
Campbell, B., and L. Barry, 'The population geography of Great
Britain *c.*1290: a provisional reconstruction', in C. Briggs,
P. M. Kitson and S. J. Thompson (eds), *Population, Welfare and
Economic Change in Britain, 1290–1834* (Woodbridge, 2014),
pp. 43–78.
Campbell B., and M. Overton, 'A New Perspective on Medieval and
Early Modern Agriculture: Six Centuries of Norfolk Farming,
*c.*1250–*c.*1850', *P&P*, 141 (1993), 38–105.
Carr, A. D., 'Wales: economy and society', in S.H. Rigby (ed.),
A Companion to Britain in the Later Middle Ages (Oxford, 2003),
pp. 125–41.
Carr, A. D., *Medieval Anglesey*, 2nd edn (Llangefni, 2011).
Carr, A. D., *The Gentry of North Wales in the Later Middle Ages*
(Cardiff, 2017).
Chapman, A., *Welsh Soldiers in the Middle Ages, 1282–1422*
(Woodbridge, 2015).
Clark, G., 'The Long March of History: Farm Wages, Population,
and Economic Growth, England 1209–1869', *EcHR*, 60 (2007),
97–135.
Coghlan, A., 'Roman Invasion Left No Genetic Legacy', *New Scientist*,
225/3013 (2015), 10–11.
Crouch, D., 'The transformation of medieval Gwent', in *GwentCH*,
pp. 1–45.

Davies, M., 'Field systems of south Wales', in A. R. H. Baker and R. A. Butlin (eds), *Studies of Field Systems in the British Isles* (Cambridge, 1973), pp. 480–529.

Davies, R. R., 'The Survival of the Bloodfeud in Medieval Wales', *History*, 54 (1969), 338–57.

Davies, R. R., 'The social structure of medieval Glamorgan', in *GlamCH*, pp. 285–97.

Davies, R. R., *Lordship and Society in the March of Wales, 1282–1400* (Oxford, 1978).

Davies, R. R., *The Age of Conquest: Wales, 1063–1415* (Oxford, 1991).

Davies, R. R., *The Revolt of Owain Glyn Dŵr* (Oxford, 1995).

Davies, R. R., 'Plague and revolt', *GwentCH*, pp. 217–40.

Davies, W., *Wales in the Early Middle Ages* (Leicester, 1982).

Dimmock, S., 'Urban and Commercial Networks in the Later Middle Ages: Chepstow, Severnside and the Ports of Southern Wales', *Archaeologia Cambrensis*, 152 (2003), 53–68.

Dimmock, S., 'The Custom Book of Chepstow', *Studia Celtica*, 38 (2004), 131–49.

Dimmock, S., 'Haverfordwest: An Exemplar for the Study of Southern Welsh Towns in the Later Middle Ages', *WHR*, 22 (2004), 1–28.

Dimmock, S., 'Reassessing the Towns of Southern Wales in the Later Middle Ages', *Urban History*, 32 (2005), 33–45.

Dimmock, S., 'The Origins of Welsh Apprentices in Sixteenth-century Bristol', *WHR*, 24 (2008–9), 116–40.

Dimmock, S., *The Origin of Capitalism in England, 1400–1600* (Leiden, 2014).

Down, K., 'Colonial society and economy in the high Middle Ages', in A. Cosgrove (ed.), *A New History of Ireland, II: Medieval Ireland, 1169–1534* (Oxford, 1993), pp. 439–91.

Duffy, S., 'The Welsh conquest of Ireland', in E. Purcell, P. MacCotter, J. Nyhan and J. Sheehan (eds), *Clerics, Kings and Vikings: Essays on Medieval Ireland in Honour of Donnchadh Ó Corráin* (Dublin, 2015), pp. 103–14.

Dyer, C., *Standards of Living in the Later Middle Ages: Social Change in England, c.1200–1520*, revised edn (Cambridge, 1998).

Dyer, C., *Making a Living in the Middle Ages: The People of Britain, 850–1520* (London, 2002).

Dyer, C., 'A Golden Age rediscovered: labourers' wages in the fifteenth century', in M. Allen and D. Coffman (eds), *Money Prices and Wages: Essays in Honour of Professor Nicholas Mayhew* (Houndmills, 2015), pp. 180–95.

Dykes, D. M., 'Seventeenth-century Glamorgan Trade Tokens', *Morgannwg*, 10 (1966), 31–51.

Emery, F. V., 'West Glamorgan Farming, circa 1580–1620, [part] I', *NLWJ*, 9 (1956), 392–400.

Emery, F. V., 'West Glamorgan Farming, circa 1580–1620, [part] II', *NLWJ*, 10 (1957), 17–34.

Evans, H. T, *Wales and the Wars of the Roses* (Stroud, repr. 1995).

Farmer, D. L., 'Prices and wages, 1350–1500', in E. Miller (ed.), *AgHist.*, vol. III: *1348–1500* (Cambridge, 1991), pp. 431–525.

Finberg, H. P. R. (ed.), *AgHist.*, vol. I, part II: *A.D. 43–1042* (Cambridge, 1972).

Fleming, P., 'The Severn Sea: urban networks and connections in the fifteenth century', in E. T. Jones and R. Stone (eds), *The World of the Newport Medieval Ship: Trade, Politics and Shipping in the Mid-fifteenth Century* (Cardiff, 2018), pp. 116–33

Fulton, H. (ed.), *Urban Culture in Medieval Wales* (Cardiff, 2012).

Given, J., 'The Economic Consequences of the English Conquest of Gwynedd', *Speculum*, 74 (1989), 11–45.

Goldberg, P. J. P., *Women, Work, and Life Cycle in a Medieval Economy: Women in York and Yorkshire, c.1300–1520* (Oxford, 1992).

Gray, H. L., *English Field Systems* (Cambridge, Mass., 1915).

Griffiths, R.A., 'The medieval boroughs of Glamorgan and medieval Swansea, I: The boroughs of the lordship of Glamorgan', in *GlamCH*, pp. 333–78.

Griffiths, R. A. (ed.), *Boroughs of Medieval Wales* (Cardiff, 1978).

Griffiths, R. A., 'Carmarthen', in *Boroughs*, pp. 130–63.

Griffiths, R. A., 'Medieval Severnside: the Welsh connection', in R. R. Davies, R. A. Griffiths, I. G. Jones and K. O. Morgan (eds),

Welsh Society and Nationhood: Historical Essays Presented to Glanmor Williams (Cardiff, 1984), pp. 70–89.

Griffiths, R. A., 'Wales and the Marches', in D. Palliser (ed.), *The Cambridge Urban History of Britain*, vol. 1 (Cambridge, 2000), pp. 681–714.

Griffiths, R. A., 'After Glyn Dŵr: An Age of Reconciliation?', *Proceedings of the British Academy*, 117 (2002), 139–164.

Griffiths, R. A., 'William Rees and the modern study of medieval Wales', in R. A. Griffiths and P. R. Schofield (eds), *Wales and the Welsh in the Middle Ages: Essays Presented to J. Beverly Smith* (Cardiff, 2011), pp. 203–20.

Grigg, D. B., *Population Growth and Agrarian Change: An Historical Prospective* (Cambridge, 1980).

Guest, P., 'The Early Monetary History of Roman Wales: Identity, Conquest and Acculturation on the Imperial Fringe', *Britannia*, 39 (2008), 33–58.

Hallam, H. E. (ed.) *AgHist.*, vol. II: *1042–1350* (Cambridge, 1988).

Hatcher, J., and M. Bailey, *Modelling the Middle Ages: The History and Theory of England's Economic Development* (Oxford, 2001).

Hatcher, J., 'Unreal wages: long-run living standards and the "Golden Age" of the fifteenth century', in B. Dodds and C. D. Liddy (eds), *Commercial Activity, Markets and Entrepreneurs in the Middle Ages* (Woodbridge, 2011), pp. 1–24.

Hilton, R. H., 'Peasant Movements in England before 1381', *EcHR*, 2nd series, 2 (1949–50), 117–36.

Hilton, R. H., *Bond Men Made Free: Medieval Peasant Movements and the English Rising of 1381* (London, 1973).

Hilton, R. H., *The English Peasantry in the Later Middle Ages: The Ford Lectures for 1973 and Related Studies* (Oxford, 1975).

Hilton, R. H., 'A Crisis of Feudalism', *P&P*, 80 (1978), 3–19.

Hilton, R. H., 'Small Town Life in England before the Black Death', *P&P*, 105 (1984), 53–78.

Hilton, R. H., 'Low-level urbanization: the seigneurial borough of Thornbury in the Middle Ages', in Z. Razi and R. Smith (eds), *Medieval Society and the Manor Court* (Oxford, 1996), pp. 482–517.

Holden, B., *Lords of the Central Marches: English Aristocracy and Frontier Society, 1087–1265* (Oxford, 2008).

Holmes, W., 'The Future of Animals as Sources of Human Food', *Proceedings of the Nutritional Society*, 29 (1970), 237–44.

Howell, R., 'Roman Past and Medieval Present: Caerleon as a Focus for Continuity and Conflict in the Middle Ages', *Studia Celtica*, 46 (2012), 1–21.

Howells, J., 'The countryside', in R. F. Walker (ed.), *Pembrokeshire County History*, vol. II: *Medieval Pembrokeshire* (Haverfordwest, 2002), pp. 401–25.

Hurley, C., 'Landscapes of Gwent and the Marches as seen through the charters of the seventh to eleventh centuries', in N. Edwards (ed.), *Landscape and Settlement in Medieval Wales* (Oxford, 1997), pp. 31–40.

Jack, R. I., 'The Cloth Industry in Medieval Wales', *WHR*, 10 (1980–1), 443–60.

Jack, R. I., 'New settlement: H Wales and the Marches', in E. H. Hallman (ed.), *AgHist.*, *vol. II: 1042–1350* (Cambridge, 1988), pp. 260–71.

Jack, R. I., 'I. Farming techniques: H Wales and the Marches', in H. E. Hallman (ed.), *AgHist.*, vol. II: *1042–1350* (Cambridge, 1988), pp. 412–96.

Jack, R. I, 'Social structure: H Wales and the Marches', in H. E. Hallman (ed.), *AgHist.*, vol. II: *1042–1350* (Cambridge, 1988), pp. 699 714.

Jenkins, D., 'Property interests in the classical Welsh law of women', in D. Jenkins and M. E. Owen (eds), *The Welsh Law of Women* (Cardiff, 1980), pp. 69–92.

Johnson, L., 'Amobr and amobrwyr: The Collection of Marriage Fees and Sexual Fines in Late Medieval Wales', *TransCymm.*, 18 (2012), 10–21.

Johnston, D., 'Towns in medieval Welsh poetry', in *UrbanCult.*, pp. 95–115.

Jones, E. T. and R. Stone, (eds), *The World of the Newport Medieval Ship: Trade, Politics and Shipping in the Mid-fifteenth Century* (Cardiff, 2018).

Jones, G. R. J., 'The Distribution of Medieval Settlement in Anglesey', *TransAng.* (1955), 27–96.

Jones, G. R. J., 'The Tribal System in Wales: A Re-assessment in the Light of Settlement Studies', *WHR*, 1 (1960–3), 111–32.

Jones, G. R. J., 'Post-Roman Wales', in H. P. R. Finberg (ed.), *AgHist.*, vol. I, part II: *A.D. 43–1042* (Cambridge, 1972), pp. 283–382.

Jones Pierce, T., 'Landlords in Wales, nobility and gentry', in H. P. R. Finberg (ed.), *AgHist.*, vol. IV: *1500–1640* (Cambridge, 1967), pp. 357–81.

Jones Pierce, T., *Medieval Welsh Society: Selected Essays*, ed., J. B. Smith (Cardiff, 1972).

Jones Pierce, T., 'The growth of commutation in Gwynedd in the thirteenth century', in *WelshSoc.*, pp. 103–26.

Jones Pierce, T., 'A Caernarvonshire manorial borough', in *WelshSoc.*, pp. 127–93.

Jones Pierce, T., 'The gafael in Bangor MS 1939', in *WelshSoc.*, pp. 195–228.

Jones Pierce, T., 'Medieval settlement in Anglesey', in *WelshSoc.*, pp. 251–87.

Jones Pierce, T., 'Medieval Cardiganshire – a study in social origins', in *WelshSoc.*, pp. 309–27.

Jones Pierce, T., 'Pastoral and agricultural settlements in early Wales', in *WelshSoc.*, pp. 339–51.

Jordan, W. C., *The Great Famine: Northern Europe in the Early Fourteenth Century* (Princeton, 1996).

Kershaw, I., 'The Great Famine and Agrarian Crisis in England, 1315–1322', *P&P*, 59 (1973), 3–50.

Kissock, J., 'Some Examples of Co-axial Field Systems in Pembrokeshire', *BBCS*, 40 (1993), 190–7.

Kissock, J., 'Settlement and society', in *GwentCH*, pp. 70–88.

Kowaleski, M., 'The Commercialization of the Sea Fisheries in Medieval England and Wales', *International Journal of Maritime History*, 15 (2003), 177–231.

Kreckel, R., 'Dimensions of Social Inequality – Conceptual Analysis and Theory of Society', *Sociologische Gids*, 23 (1976), 338–62.

Langdon, J., and J. Masschaele, 'Commercial Activity and Population Growth in Medieval England', *P&P*, 190 (2006), 35–81.

Letters, S., et al. (eds), *Gazetteer of Markets and Fairs in England and Wales to 1516*, 2 vols, List and Index Society, special series, 32 and 33 (Kew, 2003).

Lewis, E. A., 'The development of industry and commerce in Wales during the Middle Ages', *TransRoyal*, new series, 17 (1903), 121–73.

Lewis, E. A., *The Medieval Boroughs of Snowdonia* (London, 1912).

Lewis, E. A., 'A Contribution to the Commercial History of Medieval Wales', *Y Cymmrodor*, 24 (1913), 86–188.

Lieberman, M., *The March of Wales, 1067–1300* (Cardiff, 2008).

Lilley, K. D., *Urban Life in the Middle Ages, 1000–1450* (Basingstoke, 2002).

Lloyd, J. E., *A History of Wales from the Earliest Times to the Edwardian Conquest*, 2 vols (London, 1911).

Longley, D., 'Medieval Settlement and Landscape Change on Anglesey', *Landscape History*, 23 (2001), 39–59.

Longley, D., 'Hafoty and its Occupiers', *TransAng.* (2007), 25–39.

Longley, D., 'Gwynedd before and after the conquest', in D. M. Williams and J. R. Kenyon (eds), *The Impact of the Edwardian Castles in Wales* (Oxford, 2010), pp. 16–32.

Malthus, T. R., *An Essay on the Principle of Population* (London 1798).

Marx, K. and Engels, F., *The Communist Manifesto*, ed. J. C. Isaac (London, 2012).

McCormick, F., 'The Decline of the Cow: Agriculture and Settlement Change in Early Medieval Ireland', *Peritia*, 20 (2008), 209–24.

McFarlane, K. B., *The Nobility of Later Medieval England: The Ford Lectures for 1953 and Related Studies* (Oxford, 1973).

McNally, D., *Political Economy and the Rise of Capitalism: A Reinterpretation* (Berkeley, 1988).

Miller, E. (ed.), *AgHist.*, vol. III: *1348–1500* (Cambridge, 1991).

Miller, E. and Hatcher, J., *Medieval England: Rural Society and Economic Change, 1086–1348* (London, 1978).

Miller, E., and Hatcher, J., *Medieval England: Towns, Commerce, and Crafts, 1086-1348* (London, 1995).

Nelson, L. H., *The Normans in South Wales, 1070-1171* (London, 1966).

Nightingale, P., 'England and the European Depression of the Mid-fifteenth Century', *The Journal of European Economic History*, 26 (1997), 631-56.

Overton, M., and B. Campbell, 'Norfolk Livestock Farming 1250-1740: A Comparative Study of Manorial Accounts and Probate Inventories', *Journal of Historical Geography*, 18 (1992), 377-96.

Owen, D. H., 'The Englishry of Denbigh: An English Colony in Medieval Wales', *TransCymm.* (1974/5), 57-76.

Owen, D. H., 'The occupation of the land: F Wales and the Marches', in E. Miller (ed.), *AgHist.*, vol. III, *1348-1500* (Cambridge, 1991), pp. 92-106.

Owen, D. H., 'Farming practice and techniques: F Wales and the Marches', in E. Miller (ed.), *AgHist.*, vol. III: *1348-1500* (Cambridge, 1991), pp. 238-54.

Owen, D. H., 'Tenant farming and tenant farmers: F Wales and the Marches', in E. Miller (ed.), *AgHist.*, vol. III: *1348-1500* (Cambridge, 1991), pp. 648-61.

Palliser, D., 'Introduction', in D. Palliser (ed.), *Cambridge Urban History of Britain*, vol. I: *c.600-1540* (Cambridge, 2000), pp. 1-16.

Platt, C., *The English Medieval Town* (London, 1976).

Poos, L., 'Life Expectancy and "Age of First Appearance" in Medieval Manorial Court Rolls', *Local Population Studies*, 37 (1986), 45-52.

Postan, M. M., 'Village Livestock in the Thirteenth Century', *EcHR*, 15 (1962), 219-49.

Postan, M. M. (ed.), *The Cambridge Economic History of Europe, vol. I: The Agrarian Life of the Middle Ages*, 2nd edn (Cambridge, 1972).

Postan, M. M., 'England', in M. M. Postan (ed.), *The Cambridge Economic History of Europe, vol. I: The Agrarian Life of the Middle Ages*, 2nd edn (Cambridge, 1972), pp. 549-632.

Postan, M. M., *The Medieval Economy and Society: An Economic History of Britain in the Middle Ages* (London, 1972/ Harmondsworth, 1975).

Powell, N. M. W., '"Near the margin of existence?" Upland Prosperity in Wales during the Early Modern Period', *Studia Celtica*, 41 (2007), 137–62.

Pryce, H., *J. E. Lloyd and the Creation of Welsh History: Renewing a Nation's Past* (Cardiff, 2011).

Pugh, T. B., 'The marcher lords of Glamorgan and Morgannwg, 1317–1485', in *GlamCH*, pp. 167–204.

Rees, E. A., *Welsh Outlaws and Bandits: Political Rebellion and Lawlessness in Wales, 1400–1603* (Kings Norton, 2001).

Rees, W., 'The Black Death in Wales', *TransRoyal*, 4th series, 3 (1920), 115–35.

Rees, W., *South Wales and the March, 1284–1415: A Social and Agrarian Study* (Oxford, 1924).

Rees, W., 'South Wales and the March in the fourteenth century', map, four sheets (Ordinance Survey, 1933).

Richards, M., *Welsh Administrative and Territorial Units: Medieval and Modern* (Cardiff, 1969).

Ridolfi, L., 'L'histoire immobile? Six Centuries of Real Wages in France from Louis IX to Napoleon III: 1250–1860', *LEM Working Paper Series* (2017/14), www.lem.sssup.it/wplem.html.

Rigby, S. H., '[Book review] Christopher Dyer, *Making a Living in the Middle Ages: The People of Britain, 850–1520*', *Social History*, 15 (1990), 111–14.

Rigby, S. H., *English Society in the Later Middle Ages: Class, Status and Gender* (Houndmills, 1995).

Rigby, S. H., 'Historical Causation: Is One Thing More Important than Another?' *History*, 80 (1995), 227–42.

Rigby, S. H. (ed.), *A Companion to Britain in the Later Middle Ages* (Oxford, 2003).

Rigby, S. H., 'Historical Materialism: Social Structure and Social Change in the Middle Ages', *Journal of Medieval and Early Modern Studies*, 34 (2004), 473–522.

Rigby, S. H., 'Introduction: social structure and economic change in late medieval England', in R. Horrox and W. M. Ormrod (eds), *A Social History of England, 1200–1500* (Cambridge, 2006).

Rigby, S. H., *Boston, 1086–1225: A Medieval Boom Town* (Lincoln, 2017).

Rippon, S., 'Wetland reclamation on the Gwent Levels: dissecting a historic landscape', in N. Edwards (ed.), *Landscape and Settlement in Medieval Wales* (Oxford, 1997), pp. 13–40.

Rippon, S., C. Smart and B. Pears, T*he Fields of Britannia: Community and Change in the Late Roman and Early Medieval Landscape* (Oxford, 2015).

Robinson, D. M., *Cowbridge: The Archaeology and Topography of a Small Market Town in the Vale of Glamorgan* (Swansea, 1980).

Runciman, W. G., *A Treatise on Social Theory, vol. 2: Substantive Social Theory* (Cambridge, 1989).

Schofield, P. R., 'The family and the village community', in S. H. Rigby (ed.), *A Companion to Britain in the Later Middle Ages* (Oxford, 2003), pp. 26–46.

Schofield, P. R., 'Wales and the Great Famine of the Early Fourteenth Century', *WHR*, 29 (2018), 143–67.

Seebohm, F. A., *The Tribal System in Wales: Being an Inquiry into the Structure and Methods of Tribal Society* (London, 1895).

Slavin, P., 'The fifth rider of the apocalypse: the great cattle plague in England and Wales and its economic consequences, 1319–50', in S. Cavaciocchi (ed.), *Le Interazioni fra Economia e Ambiente Biologico nell'Europa Preindustriale, secc. XIII–XVIII* (Florence, 2010), pp. 165–79.

Slavin, P., 'The Great Bovine Pestilence and its Economic and Environmental Consequences in England and Wales', *EcHR*, 65 (2012), 1239–66.

Smith, J. B., 'Crown and Community in the Principality of North Wales in the Reign of Henry Tudor', *WHR*, 3 (1966), 145–71.

Smith, Ll. B., 'The Gage and the Land Market in Medieval Wales', *EcHR*, 29 (1976), 537–50.

Smith, Ll. B., 'Tir Prid: Deeds of Gage of Land in Late-medieval Wales', *BBCS*, 27 (1977), 263–77.
Smith, Ll. B., 'Seignorial Income in the Fourteenth Century: The Arundels in Chirk', *BBCS*, 28 (1979), 443–57.
Smith, Ll. B., 'The Statute of Wales, 1284', *WHR*, 10 (1980–1), 127–54.
Smith, Ll. B., 'Towards a history of women in late medieval Wales', in M. Roberts and S. Clarke (eds), *Women and Gender in Early Modern Wales* (Cardiff, 2000), pp. 14–49.
Smith, Ll. B., 'A Contribution to the History of Galanas in Late-medieval Wales', *Studia Celtica*, 43 (2009), 87–94.
Smith, Ll. B., 'Family, Land and Inheritance in Late Medieval Wales: A Case Study of Llannerch in the Lordship of Dyffryn Clwyd', *WHR*, 27 (2015), 417–58.
Smith, P., *Houses of the Welsh Countryside: A Study in Historical Geography* (London, 1975).
Soulsby, I., *The Towns of Medieval Wales: A Study of their History, Archaeology and Early Topography* (Chichester, 1983).
Stephenson, D., 'The medieval borough of Caersws: origin and decline', *Montgomeryshire Collections*, 102 (2014), 103–9.
Stephenson, D., *Medieval Powys: Kingdom, Principality and Lordships, 1132–1293* (Woodbridge, 2016).
Stephenson, D., *Medieval Wales, c.1050–1332: Centuries of Ambiguity* (Cardiff, 2019).
Stevens, M. F., *Urban Assimilation in Post-conquest Wales: Ethnicity, Gender and Economy in Ruthin, 1282–1348* (Cardiff, 2010).
Stevens, M. F., 'Anglo-Welsh towns of the early fourteenth century: a survey of urban origins, property-holding and ethnicity', in *UrbanCult.*, pp. 137–62.
Stevens, M. F., 'The Great Famine in Dyffryn Clwyd, 1315–22', *DHST*, 63 (2015), 13–35.
Stevens, M. F. and R. Czaja, 'The place of native populations in the chartered towns of conquered regions: Wales and Prussia as a comparative case study' (forthcoming).
Suggett, R., 'The interpretation of late medieval houses in Wales', in R. R. Davies and G. H. Jenkins (eds), *From Medieval to Modern*

Wales: Historical Essays in Honour of Kenneth O. Morgan and Ralph A. Griffiths (Cardiff, 2004), pp. 81–103.

Taylor, A. J., *The Welsh Castles of Edward I* (London, 1986).

Taylor, D., *Watermills of the Lordship of Gower* (Bishopston, 2009).

Thomas, C., 'Thirteenth-century Farm Economies in North Wales', *Agricultural History Review*, 16 (1968), 1–14.

Thomas, C., 'Field Name Evidence in the Reconstruction of Medieval Settlement Nuclei in North Wales', *NLWJ*, 21 (1980), 340–56.

Thomas, C., 'A Cultural-ecological Model of Agrarian Colonization in Upland Wales', *Landscape History*, 14 (1992), 37–50.

Verhulst, A., 'The Origins and Early Development of Medieval Towns in Northern Europe', *EcHR*, 47 (1994), 362–73.

Wade-Evans, A. W., *Welsh Medieval Law: Being a Text of the Laws of Howel the Good* (Oxford, 1909).

Walker, D., 'Cardiff', in *Boroughs*, pp. 102–28.

Walker, D., *Medieval Wales* (Cambridge, 1990).

Ward, S. W., 'A Survey of Holt–Farndon Medieval Bridge', *Cheshire Past: An Annual Review of Archaeology in Cheshire*, 1 (1992), 14–15.

Watkin, T. G., *The Legal History of Wales*, 2nd edn (Cardiff, 2012).

Williams, G., *Renewal and Reformation Wales, c.1415–1642* (Oxford, 1993).

Ziegler, P., *The Black Death*, 2nd edn (London, 1998).

INDEX

Aberarth, 57
Abergavenny, 39
Abergwili, 60, 63
Aberystwyth, 34, 41, 57-8, 92
alienation, land, 81-2, 115
amobr, 67, 89-90, 120
Anglesey, 14, 28, 30, 32, 57, 61, 81-3, 85, 88, 93
Anglo-Normans, 4, 16-18, 20-2, 28, 31, 33, 37, 39, 41, 58, 91, 107-8
Annales school, 4
apprenticeship, 95, 119
arable acres, total in Wales and England, 23

Bailey, Mark, 6, 21, 105
bailiff, 15, 89
Bangor
  Bishop of, 57
  borough, 60
bastardy, 79-80

beadle (*see also* bailiff), 15
beans (*see also* cereals), 34, 56
Beaumaris, 41, 58, 60, 94
Black Death *see* plague
Bloch, Marc, 113
Bolton, Jim, 1, 39
bondmen *see* serfdom
boroughs, 39-43, 59-65, 90-2, 94
  historiography, 5
  liberties, 40-1, 90
Brecon, lordship, 34, 37, 59, 68, 70, 87, 118
Brenner, Robert, 113-14
Bristol, 16, 56-7, 59, 61, 63, 92, 94-5
Britnell, Richard, 1-2, 65, 117
Broadberry, Stephen, 2, 24
Bromfield and Yale, 69, 79-80
Builth, 68
Bulkeleys, of Anglesey, 94
Butler, Lawrence, 5

Caerleon, 16
Caernarfon, 16, 60-1, 63
Caernarfonshire, 41
Caldicot, 31, 84, 87
Campbell, Bruce, 2, 24, 36, 53, 119
cantref, 13-14
Cantref Mawr, 14
capital, 54, 69, 82, 84, 88, 119
  human, 63, 119
capitalism, agrarian, 114
Caradog ap Gruffudd, 17
Cardiff, 16, 31, 39, 60, 62-3, 65
Cardiganshire, 14-15, 19, 28, 33, 57
Carew Castle, 94
Carmarthen, New (staple), 39-40, 58, 60-3, 65, 92
Carmarthen, Old, 60, 63
carpenters, 54, 60, 94
Carr, Antony, 2-3, 21, 82, 85, 93, 106
Castell y Bere, 41
castles, 20, 26, 39, 41-2, 62, 69, 85, 91
cereals, 24, 27, 36, 56, 86, 88, 111
  barley, 34, 37, 56
  oats, 34, 36-7, 56, 83-4, 86
  prices, 36, 83, 85-7, 107, 111
  wheat, 23-4, 27, 34, 36-7, 55-6, 84, 86
Chepstow, 17, 20, 39, 61, 63, 92, 95
Chester, 16, 56-7, 94
children, 80, 108, 111
Chirk, lordship, 68-70, 79, 88-9
churches, 41-2, 62
church wealth, 38
Cilgerran, 62
class conflict, 112-16
climate, 3, 21, 107, 119
cloth industry, 32, 58-9, 94-5, 118
Clun, 59, 79

coal (sea coal), 54, 57
colonisation (*see also* immigration)
  rural, 26-38
  urban, 39-43, 62-5
commercialisation, 4, 6, 39-42, 64, 78, 116-19
commercialisation model, 116-19
common land, fields (*see also* field systems), 20
commorth, 68
commotes, 13-15
commutation, 33, 38-9, 41, 64, 68, 109-10
conquest of Wales, 17, 27, 33, 39, 41, 54, 77, 85, 88, 112, 120
Conwy, 41, 93
corvisers, 119
court *see* law
Cowbridge, 63, 87
credit, 57, 82
Cricieth, 90
customs accounts, 60

Dafydd ap Gwilym, 61
dairy, 21, 24-5, 37, 56, 84, 111
Davies, Sir Robert Rees, 5, 30, 33, 67, 69, 87, 93
death duties, 67
de Clare, of Glamorgan, 37
de Grey, Reginald, 79
Deheubarth, 6, 13, 19, 33
de Lacy, Henry, 32
demesne lands (*tir bwrdd*) (*see also* field systems), 15, 27-8, 69, 87, 110, 112-13, 115
demographics
  demographic change, 2, 6, 18, 21-5, 29-35, 56, 65, 87, 91, 106-14, 117, 121
  demographic model, 106-11, 117

Denbigh
 borough, 47, 64, 91
 lordship, 32, 77, 93
 depression, pan-European
  see economy, depression,
  pan-European
diet, 36, 56, 84, 111
Dinefwr, 91
Dolforwyn, 91
dower, 79–80
drapers, 94
dyers, 59
Dyffryn Clwyd, 34, 36, 83, 85–6, 91

economy
 decline, 87–93
 depression, pan-European, 91,
  94, 107, 119
 growth, 23–4, 29, 35, 37, 42–3,
  54, 65–6, 108–10, 116–19
Edward I, 40–2, 56, 58, 60, 81, 85,
 90
Edward II, 60, 89
Edward III, 90
enclosure, 29, 83
Englishries, 26–9, 31, 34, 38, 53, 55,
 83–4, 88, 93
escheat, 32, 77, 80–1, 112, 115
ethnicity, Welsh, 28–9, 32–3, 41,
 63, 72, 79, 81–2, 89–91, 93–4,
 116, 120

family, structure, 18, 93, 107
famine, 22, 35, 77, 82–4, 90, 106–7,
 110–11
farm of office (i.e. lease of office), 26,
 67–8, 89
feudalism
 crisis of, 113–15
 in Welsh society, 14

field systems, 20, 22–5, 29, 31,
 34–6, 85
 infield-outfield, 24, 35
 land reclamation, 31
 open fields (*tir cyfrif*), 14, 20–1,
  27–8, 83, 108
 three-field, 34–5
 transhumance, 18, 20, 28
 two-field, 34–6
fisheries, 26, 55, 57–8
fitz Alan, Richard II, 69
fitz Osbern, William, 17, 20, 26,
 39–41, 43, 61, 121
Flemings, 32
Flint, 57, 90
Flintshire, 34, 57
forester, 26, 89
fulling, mills (*see also* mills), 58,
 118
Fulton, Helen, 5

galanas, 78–80
gentry *see* squirearchy
Gerald of Wales, 20, 32
Glamorgan, lordship, 26, 28, 31, 37,
 56–7, 62, 66, 88, 91, 94
Gloucester, 56–7, 94
Glyndŵr, Owain, 6–7, 63, 83, 91–2,
 118–19
Glywysing, 13, 28
Godwinson, Harold, 17
Gower, 36, 56, 58
grain *see* cereals
Gray, Howard, 35
Gruffydd ap Llywelyn, 17
gwely, 18–20, 24–5, 28–9, 66,
 77–83, 93, 108, 112, 120
Gwendraeth Fach, river, 91
Gwent, 5, 17, 20, 31, 34, 39, 93,
 116, 121

Gwent Levels, 31
gwestfa, 14–16, 19
Gwynedd, 13, 19, 36–7, 39, 58, 66

Hafoty House, 94
Hanmers, of Maelor Saesneg (Flintshire), 94
harbours *see* ports
Harlech, 90, 92
Hatcher, John, 1, 6, 105
Haverfordwest, 32, 58, 60, 63, 95
Henblas, Beaumaris, 94
Henry II, 56
Henry IV, 92
Henry VII, 95
Henry VIII, 95, 121
Hereford, 41, 56–7, 59, 66, 94
Herefordshire, 36–7, 56
herring (*see also* fisheries), 58
Hilton, Rodney, 113
Holt, 58, 63
Holywell, 57
housing, 14, 20, 57, 94
Hundred Years' War, 7, 91
Hywel Dda *see* law, Welsh

immigration (*see also* colonisation)
    English, rural, 27–9, 31–4, 90, 109, 120
    English, urban, 39–43, 62–5, 109
    Welsh, 94–5, 119
income, seigniorial, 22, 42, 65–70, 87–90, 93, 113
industry, 7, 53–4, 59, 70–3, 92, 102, 117, 124, 136
infrastructure, 58, 85
inheritance, 41, 79–81, 83, 108
    female, 80–1
    partible, 81, 108
investment, 42, 58, 69, 92

Ireland, 1–2, 16, 33, 41, 53, 95
iron mines, 57

Jack, Ian, 5, 21, 35
Jones, Glanville, 4, 19, 21
Jones Pierce, Thomas, 4–6, 17, 19, 21

Kenfig, 91

labour, 14, 16, 21, 27, 39, 41–2, 59, 84–9, 107, 111–13, 116–18
labour market, 87–9
services, 14, 16, 27, 39, 41, 85, 116, 118
Lampeter, 62
land *see* field systems
Landsker line, 32
law, 4, 13, 15, 26, 41, 66, 69, 77–82
    common law, 67, 113
    courts, 15, 26, 41, 66–7, 69, 79
    criminal, 67, 78–80
    English legal process, 67, 79, 82
    urban, 41
    Welsh, 13, 67, 78–82, 89–90
lead mines, 57
lease, land and structures (*see also* farm of office), 26, 81–3, 88, 93
leather, 59
Lewis, Edward Arthur, 3, 5, 40, 54–5, 117
livestock
    cattle, 20, 23–4, 37–8, 56, 59, 68, 70, 79, 86–7
    prices, 86–7
    horses, 37–8
    murrain, 82, 84, 111
    sheep, 37–8, 56, 59, 68
Llandaff, Bishop of, 22
Llangadog, 62

Llanidloes, 62
Llannerch, Dyffryn Clwyd, 34, 93
llys, 15
Llywelyn ap Gruffydd, 41
Longley, David, 83
lordship, 14, 26–8, 65–70, 88–9, 115
  courts (*see also* law, courts), 66, 79, 82
  heavy-handed, 67–70, 87–8, 115
  judicial, 66–9, 87, 111, 115
  revenues *see* income, seigniorial
Ludlow, 59
luxuries, goods, 16, 70

Machynlleth, 42
maenor, 13–14, 16, 18
maerdref, 15
Malthusian *see* demographic model
Manorbier, 20, 27
manors, 26–7, 69, 84, 87, 118
margin, 'marginal' agriculture, 18, 21, 29, 36–7, 66, 68, 108–9
markets, 16–17, 20, 24, 42, 53, 62, 64–5, 86, 94, 116–18
marriage, 67, 79–80, 89, 94, 107
Marxist model, 112–16
McCormick, Finbar, 25
Menai Strait, 57, 60
Merionethshire, 30, 41, 81, 90
Milford Haven, 95
mills, 26, 58, 69–70, 89, 118
mill stones, 27, 57
mints, 39
money/monetisation, 38–9, 41–2, 64, 67, 118–20, 129
Monmouth
  borough, 17, 20, 39, 58, 61, 64
  lordship, 68, 87
Monmouthshire, 37, 95

Monnow, river, 58
Morgannwg, 13, 28
mortality (*see also* plague), 64, 84, 106–7, 113
Mynachlog-ddu, 20, 27

Neath, 56
Nefyn, 58
Nelson, Lynn, 39
Newborough, 61, 116
Normandy, 4, 41, 113
Normans *see* Anglo-Normans
Norres, of Anglesey, 94
nucleated settlement, 14, 20, 27, 32, 58, 84

officials, 15, 26, 63, 89–90, 93, 95
Ogmore, 28–9, 88
Oswestry
  borough, 56, 94
  lordship, 79–80
Overton, 91
Owen, Huw, 5

parliament, 67, 92
pastoralism, 2, 14, 16, 21–5, 27, 29, 32, 37–8, 87, 111
Peasants' Revolt, 88, 115
Pebidiog, 32
Pembroke
  borough, 33, 39, 58
  lordship, 32, 57, 95
plague, 6, 63, 68, 77, 82–5, 87–90, 92–3, 95, 107, 110–13, 118
poetry, 61, 94
population (*see also* demographics), 2–3, 21, 23–4, 30, 33–4, 43, 53, 60–4, 68, 84–5, 91, 106–12
  urban, 59–65, 109
ports, 55, 57–8, 60–1, 63, 92, 95

Portskewett, 17
Postan, Michael, 1, 5, 38
Powys, 66
prices
  grain *see* cereals, prices
  livestock (*see also* livestock, cattle, prices), 36, 85–7, 107, 111
prid, 81–3
productivity, 32, 35–7, 53, 65, 109, 117
Pwllheli, 58

Radnor
  lordship, 27, 34
  New, borough, 31
  rape, 67, 78
Rees, William, 3–6, 26–8, 38, 40–1, 82–3, 85–6
rents, 26–7, 40–1, 63, 66–8, 88–9, 107, 114
revolt *see* Glyndŵr, Owain
rhaglaw, 15
rhinghel, 15
Rhuddlan, 39, 41, 60
Ricardo, David, 106
Rigby, Stephen, 2, 116, 119
Romans, legacy of, 16, 18, 43
Runciman, Walter, 116
Ruthin, 5, 59–60, 82, 91, 94, 118

Scotland, 2, 33, 53
Seebohm, Fredrick Arthur, 4, 19, 27
seigniorial reaction, 88–9
serfdom, 4, 15, 18–19, 27–8, 31, 37, 57, 84–5, 87–8, 107–8, 112–17
services, 14, 19, 27, 39, 67
settlement, nucleated *see* nucleated settlement
Severn, river and sea (*Môr Hafren*), 17, 22, 31

shoemakers, 119
Shrawardine Castle, 69
Shrewsbury, 56–7, 59, 94
Shropshire, 37, 56
silver, 39, 43, 54, 57, 69
Skerries Islands, 57
skinners, 59, 118
Slavin, Philip, 38, 107, 110–11
Smith, Adam, 116
Smith, Llinos, 5, 69–70, 78
smiths, 54, 60
Snowdonia, 3, 93, 117
social closure, 116, 119
soils, quality, 22–3, 30, 35–7, 108
soldiers, 16, 26, 33, 42, 69
Soulsby, Ian, 5, 43
Spain, 57, 95
squirearchy, 83–4, 90, 93–5, 97, 112
staples *see* ports
Statute of Labourers, 85
Statute of Stipends, 85
Statute of the Staple, 63, 92
Statute of Wales (Rhuddlan), 78–81, 112
St David's, Bishop of, 37
St David's, borough, 39
Striguil *see* Chepstow
subsidies *see* taxation
Swansea, 39–40

taxation, 4, 14, 19, 25, 28, 59, 66–70, 82, 90, 92, 110
  subsidies, 28, 66–7
  tithes, 38, 53
  tolls, 40–1, 58, 67, 89
  tribute, 14, 16, 27, 29, 68
Tenby, 64, 95
tenure, 80–2, 88, 93, 112, 120
  English, 78, 81–3

timber, 54, 56–7, 89
Tintern Abbey, 59
tir bwrdd see demesne lands
tir cyfrif see field systems, open fields
tithes see taxation
tolls see taxation
towns see urbanisation
Towy, river, 63
trade
    cross-border, 68, 94–5
    exports, 55–61, 68, 94
    imports, 16, 55, 61, 95
tref, 14–15
tribute see taxation
twnc, 15

unfree see serfdom
upland, 2, 18, 20–2, 24–5, 27–30, 32, 37, 56, 68, 84, 108, 121
urbanisation, 5–7, 38–43, 54–6, 60–5, 90–1, 95, 106, 109–10, 115, 117–18, 120
    urban clusters, 60, 62–3
    urban decline, 90–1
    urban population see population, urban
Usk, 63, 87

Vaughan, Henry (mayor of Bristol), 95

vetches (see also cereals), 34, 56

wages, 42, 69, 85–7, 99, 107, 111, 132
Walker, David, 68
walls, urban, 63
wealth, importance of, 25, 57, 63, 81, 90–1, 93
weather, 22, 110–11
weavers, 59, 94
Weber, Max, 116, 119
weirs (see also fisheries), 57, 69
Welshpool, 94
Welshries, 26–9, 32, 55, 59, 68, 77–83, 93, 120–1
wheelwrights, 60
White Castle, 88
Whitson, 31
Wigmore, 63
women, 59, 80, 90, 95–6, 107, 115, 123, 132, 134, 140
    Welsh, 79–81, 111–12
    widows, 80
    workers, 59, 95, 107, 111
wool, 21, 24–5, 56, 59–61
Worcester, diocese, 22–3

Yale see Bromfield and Yale

Ziegler, Philip, 84